TRUE Ghosts & Spooky Incidents

Vikas Khatri

PUSTAK MAHAL®
Delhi • Bangalore • Mumbai • Patna • Hyderabad

J-3/16 , Daryaganj, New Delhi-110002
☎ 23276539, 23272783, 23272784 • *Fax:* 011-23260518
E-mail: info@pustakmahal.com • *Website:* www.pustakmahal.com

Sales Centre

- 10-B, Netaji Subhash Marg, Daryaganj, New Delhi-110002
  ☎ 23268292, 23268293, 23279900 • *Fax:* 011-23280567
  E-mail: rapidexdelhi@indiatimes.com
- 6686, Khari Baoli, Delhi-110006
  ☎ 23944314, 23911979

Branches

Bengaluru: ☎ 080-22234025 • *Telefax:* 080-22240209
E-mail: pustak@airtelmail.in • pustak@sancharnet.in
Mumbai: ☎ 022-22010941, 022-22053387
E-mail: rapidex@bom5.vsnl.net.in
Patna: ☎ 0612-3294193 • *Telefax:* 0612-2302719
E-mail: rapidexptn@rediffmail.com
Hyderabad: *Telefax:* 040-24737290
E-mail: pustakmahalhyd@yahoo.co.in

ISBN 978-81-223-0943-0

Edition: 2012

Printed at : **Glorious Printers Delhi**

Contents

Preface

For many of us the word 'ghost' conjures up an anonymous white-robed figure, a spirit who has come back from the grave to haunt the living. These spectral beings come in a variety of forms and shapes, and some never put it in appearance at all, although they make their presence felt. They may be aimless, purposeful, playful, angelic, and even demonic.

The mechanical interpretation is that ghosts are images without substance, somehow recorded in an ethnic medium and visible under certain conditions to those of a certain cast of mind. In the psychological view of phenomena, ghosts reveal a spectrum of powerful yet understood capacities of the human mind. In fact, most believers in ghosts are probably willing to accept all of these in helping to explain a complex and varied phenomena.

Robert Graves, when asked a few years ago about the likelihood of ghosts, wrote, "The common-sense view is, I think, one should accept ghosts very much as one accepts fire — a more common but equally mysterious phenomenon. What is true? It is not really an element, not a principle motion, not a living creature — not even a disease, though a house can catch fire from its neighbours. It is an event rather than a thing or a creature. Ghosts, similarly, seem to be events rather than things or creatures."

In conclusion, I hope that this compilation will provide fresh material for discussion and enquiry among students and laymen alike. The camera, it is said, cannot lie, and though we have seen that on occasions it can be used to deceive, there is still much it has captured which defies explanation. The ghosts on these pages, I venture to suggest, prove that today such anomalies are recognised 'officially', though they are rare.

1. The Restless Skull

Collecting skulls was the private passion of a British doctor, John Kilner. He had them specially polished and encased in ebony boxes, which he displayed around his room. But the skull that fascinated him most of all was one he did not own. It was on a skeleton at West Suffolk Hospital, where he worked in the 1870s.

Part of the attraction was the skeleton's gruesome history. It was the skeleton of a murderer, 23 years old William Corder, who was hanged in public at the nearby Bury St. Edmunds Prison in April 1828 for the notorious Red Barn murder of Maria Marten.

For years, Dr. Kilner greedily eyed that skeleton as it was used to teach students. Then one night, he stole it and put it in one of the showcases in his home.

Immediately, his life became a nightmare. An evil spirit started roaming the house muttering and breathing heavily; and often sobbing was heard. Eventually, a vivid white hand floated through the air and smashed the skull's showcase.

The doctor was so horrified that he gave the skull to a friend, who was in turn subjected to so much similar terror, that he finally gave it a Christian burial. The tormented soul of killer Corder was finally able to rest in peace.

2. The Bricked-up Window

Very often ghosts are seen acting out the last moments of their lives on earth. One of the most famous examples of this is the spirit of one of America's greatest naval heroes, Stephen Decatur.

After the end of the War of Independence, Decatur got caught up in a long-running feud with one of his own comrades and challenged him to a duel.

Both men fired at the same time, but whereas Barron was only wounded, Decatur died from a shot at his lower chest.

Decatur's friends later argued that he was a marksman and could easily have killed his opponent if he had wished. But the thought of gunning down a comrade was too much for him.

A year later, Decatur's ghost was seen for the first time at the bedroom window. Since then, the window has been bricked up but his spirit apparently refuses to leave.

Some say Decatur can still be seen early on misty mornings, slipping out of his back door, a black box containing his duelling pistol tucked neatly under his arm.

3. An Emergency Call

Inspector Sid Candler of London's Metropolitan Police was called out on an emergency call on July 11, 1951. As he approached the house in Langmead Street, West Norwood, London, the Inspector vowed he would reprimand young Cecil Greenfield, who had made the emergency call, for making up tales about ghosts.

But when he met the eight members of the Greenfield family, Inspector Candler changed his mind. They were genuinely scared out of their wits. The family told him that the house had been invaded by strange flickering lights accompanied by loud noises, crashes, thumps and moans. The police stayed in the house that night, but nothing else happened.

The following night the Greenfields telephoned the police again. This time, eight constables were assigned to the house. On that night, and on subsequent visits, the police heard the noises for themselves. Apart from the noises, a shopping basket was mysteriously thrown along the hallway, cups and saucers moved of their own accord, pictures fell from the walls, a spoon rattled in the sugar bowl, lights flickered on and off by themselves, and strange footsteps were heard up and down the stairs.

Clergymen visited the house to try to exorcise the ghost, but strange things continued to happen. Mysterious footprints appeared in the loft. They were rubbed out by the police, but reappeared the following day. A radio switched itself on, and a mattress was seen floating above one of the beds. And through it all, the noises continued unabated.

The family managed to put up with the ghostly disturbances until one morning in October, when they came down to breakfast and found that all the downstairs walls had been scribbled on. They could stand it no longer and moved out of the house shortly thereafter.

When new tenants moved into the house, they were not once bothered by anything unusual. It seemed as if a poltergeist had been intent on getting rid of the Geenfields — and having achieved its objective, had returned to wherever it had come from.

4. Radio Announcer and a Ghost Hotel

Radio announcer Ray Moore, was up at 4.30 a.m. on a cold January morning in 1971. He was presenting an early morning show and was staying at the Langham Hotel, conveniently situated just across the road from the BBC studios in London. He stepped out on to his hotel room balcony, hoping the chilly air would help him to wake up, and noticed a figure at the window of the floor above. It was of a big man, wearing a uniform, and there seemed to be a glow emanating from his body.

When he went downstairs, Moore mentioned this strange apparition to the commissionaire. He was told that it was the ghost of a German officer who had killed himself by jumping out of the hotel window, just before the start of the First World War. Several other BBC personnel who have stayed in the same room on other occasions have also seen the ghost.

5. A Headless Woman

As he was driving near St. James's Park in London one morning in 1975, a taxi driver saw a headless woman crossing the road in front of him. When he reported the sighting, he was told that he had seen the ghost of an 18th century woman who had been beheaded by her husband. The murderous husband had then thrown his wife's body into the lake in St. James's Park.

6. Unexpected Visitors

A benign light, a motherless child, a witness of faultless rectitude; the following story is told by the Reverend Charles Jupp, warden of the Orphanage and Convalescent Home at Aberlour, near Craigellachie, Scotland. In 1878, he said, three young children recently orphaned by the death of their mother had been admitted to his institution. A few months later, several unexpected visitors arrived and in order to accommodate them overnight, the Reverend Jupp decided to occupy an empty bed in the children's dormitory. At breakfast the following morning, the warden told his co-workers and friends what had transpired during the night :

"As near as I can tell, I fell asleep about 11 o'clock and slept very soundly for some time. I suddenly woke without any apparent reason and felt an impulse to turn around, my face being towards the wall, from the children. Before turning, I looked up and saw a soft light in the room. The gas was burning low in the hall, and the dormitory door being open, I thought it probable that the light came from that source. It was soon evident, however, that such was not the case. I turned over, and then a wonderful vision met my gaze. Over the second bed from mine, and on the same side of the room, there was floating a small cloud of light, forming a halo of the brightness of the moon on an ordinary moonlit night."

"I sat upright in bed looking at this strange appearance, took up my watch and found the hands pointing to five minutes to one. Everything was quiet, and all the children sleeping soundly. In the bed, over which the light seemed to float, slept the youngest of the children mentioned above."

"I asked myself, 'Am I dreaming?' No! I was wide awake. I was seized with a strong impulse to rise and touch the substance, or whatever it might be (for it was about five feet high), and was getting up when something seemed to hold me back. I am certain I heard nothing, yet I felt and perfectly understood the words — 'No, lie down. It won't hurt you.' I at once did what I felt I was told to do. I fell asleep shortly afterwards and rose at half-past five, that being my usual time."

"At six, I began dressing the children, beginning at the bed farthest from the one in which I slept. Presently I came to the bed over which I had seen the light hovering. I took the little boy out, placed him on my knee, and put on some of his clothes. The child had been talking with the others; suddenly he was silent.

And then, looking me hard in the face with an extraordinary expression he said, 'Oh, Mr. Jupp, my mother came to me last night. Did you see her?' For a moment I could not answer the child. I then thought it better to pass it off, and said, 'Come, we must make haste, or we shall be late for breakfast.'"

"I never spoke of the matter to the small boy, nor did the child refer to it. Some time later, however, an account of the incident was included in the small magazine put out by the orphanage. When the boy read it, his countenance changed, and looking up he said, 'Mr. Jupp, that is me.' I said, 'Yes, that is what we saw.'

He said, 'Yes,' and then seemed to fall into deep thought, evidently with pleasant remembrances, for he smiled so sweetly to himself and seemed to forget I was present."

7. A Real Ghostwriter

Sports figures and other public personalities frequently seek assistance for their autobiographies in the form of 'ghost' writers (professional authors hired to whip their prose into shape). But real ghostwriters have plied their ethereal trade, too, as evidenced by the career of Mrs. J. H. Curran and her spiritual scribe, Patience Worth.

Curran, of St. Louis, was originally distrustful about mediums and spiritualism, but on July 8, 1913, she attended a seance in which an Ouija board was employed. Placing her hands on the board, Curran spelled out the name Patience Worth. Patience revealed herself as a 17th century English woman from Dorset, whose parents had migrated to America, where she was killed in an Indian attack.

Intrigued, Curran continued her conversations with Patience. Over the next several years, and in the course of countless sittings, a remarkable sequence of poems, stories and treatises poured from Patience, through Curran, and into print.

flowing waters. Then, suddenly, a dark-haired man appeared at the water's edge. Within seconds he was in the water alongside the boy, cradling him in his arms.

Although she had been watching him since he first appeared, Irene had not actually seen the man jump into the water. But she did not think about that at the time, for she was so relieved to have her son back safe and sound. She ran ashore to thank the stranger, but by the time she reached her son, the man was already walking away towards a nearby warehouse. When she looked again, he had disappeared. By now the dockers, who had heard her cries, were on the scene and they asked Irene why she was looking at the warehouse. When she described the person who had rescued Willem, the dockers suddenly became very quiet and asked no more about the incident.

The next day, Peter Nierman tried to find Willem's rescuer so he could thank him. After many hours of searching and asking questions, he discovered that the man who had saved his son's life was well known in the area. He was Johan Udink, a dock-worker who had drowned at that very spot—10 years ago!

13. A Ghost Dog

A small black dog was spotted by a policeman when on duty at Didsbury, Manchester, England in 1957. It was a moonlit night, and he saw the dog quite clearly in the garden of an old house. The dog walked across the lawn and then disappeared behind a tree. When the dog did not emerge from behind the tree, the policeman went to investigate. At the base of the tree was a stone on which was written: 'Paddy. Died September 2, 1913'. It was the gravestone of a dog.

14. Ballechin House

In 1876, Major Stewart died at Ballechin House in Perthshire, Scotland. He had lived there for more than 40 years and during that period had acquired something of a reputation for eccentricity. This seems to have been based on nothing more extreme than a belief in spirits, a firm conviction in the transmigration of soul, and an unusual fondness for dogs, of which he had 14 at the time of his demise. He even declared that, if possible, he wished to return to earth as the tenant of the body of a favourite black spaniel. After his death, however, his family had all 14 dogs destroyed. In doing so, they made a serious mistake.

The first signs of something amiss in the house occurred not long after the major's nephew, who had inherited the place, moved in with his wife. This lady was in the habit of balancing her housekeeping books in the room the major had used for his study. One day, busy with her books, she suddenly and quite unmistakably smelled the doggy odour in the old room. Then worse, something invisible pushed her! Somehow, she felt that whatever had pushed her was an animal. Other disquieting things happened. There were noises that could not be accounted for, knockings, explosions, and sometimes arguing voices, when no people were there.

By 1896, Ballechin House was said to be haunted. But its estates were wide, the grouse were plentiful, and the new owner, a Captain Stewart, had no difficulty that August in renting the house and shooting rights for the season to wealthy people devoted to the sport. Whether he warned them of the house's reputation is not recorded. He had acquired the house only the year before, when the old major's nephew had been knocked down and killed by a London cab.

In any case, the tenants moved in as they had paid in advance for a rental of several months. But soon they were pushed and snuffled at, and were half scared to death by animals they could not see. They stayed a few weeks and moved out, forfeiting their money.

When the marquis of Bute heard of the goings-on at Ballechin, the urge to investigate overcame him. He had a deep interest in spiritualism and was a member of the Psychical Research Society. With Captain Stewart's approval, he rented the house with a Major Le Mesurier Taylor and other members of the Society and prepared for an on-the-spot investigation.

In due course the marquis, the major, and a Miss Goodrich-Freer gathered 35 guests at Ballechin, ostensibly for a house party. Most of the guests knew nothing of Ballechin's reputation. They were soon to discover how it had been earned.

At first, the consensus among the guests was that owls and water pipes, and perhaps the servants, were making the noises. When it became obvious that the raps and muffled explosions, the sounds of shuffling feet, of quarrelling voices, and someone interminably reading aloud were too much of a production for even a forestful of owls, an army of servants, and the world's most versatile water pipes, the guests began to accuse each other. Finally, the men sat up at night in grim-jawed groups, armed with pistols and pokers.

But the ghosts of Ballechin were not deterred. Something was heard to beat powerfully against the bedroom doors, and a black spaniel, which seemed to congeal out of the very air and then melt into nothing, was seen by nearly everybody in the house.

To be nudged and sniffed at by invisible dogs and to hear invisible tails thumping the wainscot was the common lot of all the guests.

One night, a lady sharing her bedroom with another lady was awakened by the whimpering of her pet dog. She followed the animal's gaze to a bedside table. Resting on it were two black paws, each ending in thin air.

Another night, a gentleman saw a disembodied hand clutching a crucifix afloat in the air at the foot of his bed. A lone nun was seen weeping in a glen beyond the house, and then two nuns together; (possibly, the sister of the old major, who was a nun and had died 16 years before.

By the time the house party came to an end, all but one of the 35 guests were convinced that Ballechin House was haunted. Whether or not the marquis and his cohosts received thank-you notes is not recorded!

15. The Ghost of Elizabeth Hoby

A lady with a black face and hands, and wearing a long white dress haunts Bisham Abbey near Marlow in Buckinghamshire, England. She always seems to be washing her hands. It is said that this is the ghost of Lady Elizabeth Hoby, the wife of one of Queen Mary's courtiers, who murdered her son. Even now, her spirit is still trying to wash her baby's blood from her hands.

16. The Polite Ghost

The ghost of a nun knocks on the bedroom doors in Ripley Castle, Yorkshire, England. But she is very polite, and only enters the room if the occupant calls: 'Come in'!

17. A Case of Exorcism

John Willis and his wife Rosemary were watching television one evening at their home in Barking, Essex, when suddenly they heard the sound of loud crashing and banging coming from their children's room. The couple looked up in alarm and rushed upstairs to find out what was wrong.

As they entered the bedroom, an ornament crashed against the wall, narrowly missing Rosemary's head. The room itself seemed alive with activity. Bedding and toys were flying around the room. Cowering together in the corner stood their children, ten-year-old Terry and seven-year-old Sandra, terrified out of their wits.

The two children were hastily bundled out of the room, and the bedroom door was slammed shut. All four stood on the landing, shaking with fear and unable to understand what strange phenomenon could be responsible for what they had witnessed in the room.

From July to September, 1952, the Willis family had to endure a continuous barrage of similar happenings in their house.

Objects flew around rooms, a kitchen table split in half as the family looked on, an iron poker was bent in half, and the sitting-room curtains were ripped to shreds by unseen hands.

Although no one in the house was ever hurt by the poltergeist, Norman Horridge, an expert on the paranormal was convinced that a strange and evil force existed in the house, and persuaded the Willis family to agree to an exorcism.

The exorcism was carried out in September 1952. Doors blew open and banged to and fro, as if the poltergeist was angry at being banished.

Finally, the house went quiet — the poltergeist had departed for ever.

18. The Jingling Bell

Some ghosts present such a terrible sight that they are believed to frighten to death those who see them. One of the worst was the fiend of 50, Berkeley Square, London.

This apparition began to get a reputation during the 19th century. One unbeliever who scoffed at its existence was Sir Robert Warboys, who vowed to spend a night in the haunted rooms. The landlord agreed, but only if Sir Robert carried a gun. Sir Robert was also instructed to pull a cord, which rang a bell in the landlord's private apartment, if there was any trouble.

Within 45 minutes the bell was jangling violently and the landlord ran upstairs with some of Sir Robert's friends. As they approached the door, they heard a gunshot and burst in to find the would-be ghostbuster dead. There was no sign of any bullet wound. But the expression of terror on his face told its own story.

19. America's Ghost Town

Graveyards are always associated with ghosts but few can match the record of Bachelor's Grove Cemetery. This small, overgrown plot near the Rubio Woods Forest at Crestwood, Chicago, has became something of a Ghost City with more than 100 separate reports of hauntings.

Bachelor's Grove ghosts include the Hooded Monk, the White Lady and a woman seen cradling a baby.

A lake in one corner of the cemetery has its own spirit residents including a two-headed man and a farmer with his own plough — both of whom have been seen emerging on to the shore.

Some ghost hunters have reported bizarre blue and red lights weaving among the tombstones, while others experienced the touch of sweaty hands on their skin. There is even a ghostly farmhouse that grows smaller, the closer you get to it.

20. The Silent Hitchhiker

One evening in October 1979 Roy Fulton, a carpet fitter, was driving back home from a darts match in Leighton Buzzard, Bedfordshire, England. As he neared the village of Stanbridge, he stopped to pick up a young hitchhiker, a man of pale complexion, with short, curly hair, dark trousers, and a white shirt with an old-fashioned round collar. When Fulton asked him where he was going, the young man just pointed down the road. Fulton thought his passenger might be a deaf-mute and drove on in silence. After driving a mile or two, though, at a steady 45 mph, he thought a cigarette might help to break the ice, and turned to offer one to his companion.

The passenger's seat was empty. The young man had silently vanished from a moving van, whose door had never opened. Fulton drove straight to his local pub, ordered a large scotch to steady his nerves, and told his story. The landlord of the pub and the Dunstable police inspector both said later, that they believed Fulton had experienced something strange — perhaps his story was true.

21. The Haunted Office

The first unusual manifestation in the staid law office of West German attorney Sigmund Adam, 63, was the constant ringing of a telephone.

The respected attorney or his secretary would lift the receiver and there would be no one on the line. Mr. Adam informed the telephone company. "Those phones are in perfect condition," the telephone repairmen insisted.

Soon after, the pictures on the office walls began to dance to and fro in a frenzied manner. By December 18, 1967, it was virtually impossible to work in the office. Light bulbs exploded suddenly, doors opened and shut mysteriously, papers flew off the desks, and the hands of the electric clocks whirled at an increased rate of speed.

The mystified lawyer summoned the police and electricians from the Rodenheim electricity company. A careful examination of the electric lines uncovered no clues. Then someone noticed that when Adam's 19-year-old secretary passed an electric object, blue sparks flashed and sputtered.

Mr. Schneider called the University of Freilburg and requested assistance from Dr. Hans Bender, a psychologist.

Annemarie Schneider, the secretary, willingly submitted to the psychologist's extensive tests. Dr. Bender said, "Annemarie has definite psychokinetic powers. We know very little about this." Psychokinesis" is the startling ability of the mind to burst free from traditional boundaries and energise objects in a mind-over-matter manner.

Attorney Adam informed reporters that his secretary was not aware that she was creating the startling phenomena. "I understand that it's often only a temporary thing," the lawyer stated, "so I've sent Annemarie on a vacation for a few weeks."

The West German attorney was correct in his analysis of psychokinetic, or poltergeist, energy. The phenomenon starts slowly, builds to a maddening climax, and then fades away.

22. Ghost Hitchhikers

On a winter's eve in 1965, Mae Doria of Tulsa, Oklahoma, set out alone on the forty-three-mile drive to her sister's house in Pryor. "While driving on Highway 20," Doria remembered, "a few miles east of the town of Claremore, I passed a schoolhouse and saw this boy, who appeared to be around eleven or twelve years old, hitchhiking by the side of the road."

Concerned about someone so young on such a cold night, Doria pulled over and offered him a ride. "He got in the car, sat down next to me on the front seat," she said, "and we chatted about things that people who don't know each other usually talk about." Doria asked him what he was doing in the area and he said, "Playing basketball at the school." Her passenger appeared to be about five feet tall and well-built, "like a boy would look if he played sports and used his muscles." He was a Caucasian, with light-brown hair and bluish-grey eyes. But unbeknown to Mae Doria, she had just picked up a phantom hitchhiker!

The young man eventually pointed at a culvert outside Pryor and said, "Let me out over there." Not seeing any house or lights, Doria asked where he lived, to which he replied, "Over there." She was trying to determine where that might be when her passenger simply disappeared. Doria stopped the car immediately and jumped out. "I ran all around the automobile, almost hysterical," she said. "I looked everywhere, up and down the highway and to the right and left, but to no avail. He was gone." Later, Doria remembered the hitchhiker had not been wearing a jacket, despite the winter chill. A chance conversation with a utility employee two years after the event revealed that the phantom figure had first been picked up at the same spot in 1936.

An even eerier encounter involved an accidental death for which a phantom hitchhiker was at least partially responsible. In February 1951, Charles Bordeaux, of Miami, was an officer in the Air Force's Office of Special Investigations in England. An American airman had been shot and killed under mysterious circumstances, and Bordeaux was ordered to investigate.

He learnt that a security guard had spotted a man running between two parked B-36 bombers. He shouted "Halt!" three times, and when the figure refused to stop, shot at him. "I could have sworn that I hit him, but when I got to that area of the airfield, no one was there. He had disappeared." Instead, the guard's errant bullet struck and killed another airman.

Continuing his investigation, Bordeaux spoke to an officer who had also been on the flight line that fatal night. He had been driving by prior to the incident when he saw a man in a Royal Air Force uniform, hitchhiking. After the man climbed in the officer said, he asked if he could spare one of his Camel cigarettes. Then the figure asked for a lighter. The officer saw the flash of flint out of the corner of his eyes, but when he turned his head, the passenger had vanished into thin air, leaving his lighter lying on the empty seat.

23. A Ghost Bus

In the spring of 1933, a man was driving along St. Mark's Road in North Kensington, London, when he suddenly saw a double decker bus careering towards him. It was too late to avoid a collision — the bus had appeared from nowhere and all the car driver could do was to slam on his brakes and await the impact. But nothing happened. When the driver opened his eyes, the bus was nowhere in sight!

That was not the first time that the mysterious bus had been sighted. On one occasion, a driver swerved to avoid a Number 7 bus and actually crashed his car into one of the houses in the street. But when he turned to look again, the bus had disappeared.

Several other sightings of the ghostly bus were reported and a number of accidents occurred in the same street. Luckily, none of the drivers were seriously injured — until Monday, June 11, 1933, when two cars crashed head-on, killing one of the drivers. After this fatal accident, the ghost bus disappeared forever — perhaps satisfied that it had claimed at least one victim.

24. The Haunted Room

One evening in September 1912, George French and Donald Geary were returning to the farmhouse in Slieve Donard, County Down, Northern Ireland, where they were staying with friends. As they approached the building, they saw that one of the upstairs rooms was on fire. Instinctively, they rushed into the farmhouse to help.

The house did not burn down. In fact, there was no sign of any fire when they went upstairs to investigate. When the farmer, Mark Donague, came home, he told the men: "That room is haunted, so we always keep it locked. The last person to go there was one of my farm workers, ten years ago. The first I knew of it was when we heard a scream. We rushed upstairs as he staggered out of the room clutching his throat. Something in that room had tried to strangle him. The key to the room has remained in my desk drawer ever since."

The following afternoon, when Donague was out, George

and Donald went up to the room. Apart from the fact that it was dusty and the furniture decaying, the room seemed quite ordinary. Donald Geary walked in while George French stayed outside the room. The temperature dropped suddenly and a glowing ball of pink light appeared over the rocking-chair in the centre of the room. The ball of light grew larger and larger, until the whole room appeared bathed in a bright fire. The furniture began to vibrate and the rocking-chair was swaying back and forth ominously.

Suddenly Donald clutched his neck and screamed. Something was trying to strangle him. He was struggling desperately with the unseen force that was pushing him down to the floor when George rushed into the room to help his friend. As he pulled him to the door, the glow diminished and the room became warm again.

As Donald recovered in the corridor, George locked the door. They returned the key to the desk drawer and vowed not be so sceptical in the future.

25. Sinking of the *SS Violet*

Soon after the start of the Second World War, a guard on watch on the East Goodwin lightship in southern England saw an old-fashioned paddle steamer run aground on the treacherous Goodwin Sands. The guard called the Ramsgate lifeboat station, and a lifesaving crew sped to the scene. The whole area was searched, but there was no sign of any wreckage or casualties. When the guard related how the shipwreck occurred, it came to light that he had witnessed the sinking of the *SS Violet* — a steamer that had gone down many years before!

26. The Ghost Train

President Abraham Lincoln was shot dead in 1865 by John Wilkes Booth in a Washington theatre. His coffin was carried on a special funeral train, which stopped for eight minutes at each station along the route so people could pay their respects.

Soon afterwards, there were reports of a phantom train. It was draped in black and bore the President's coffin. One carriage carried a band of skeletal musicians. As the ghostly train passed along the funeral route, clocks stopped for exactly eight minutes.

27. Ghosts with a Grudge

Many old country houses are haunted by ghosts with a grudge. At Breckles Hall in Norfolk, England, it is said that a terrible scream for mercy can sometimes be heard. Doors also bang without explanation, footsteps can be heard along the passageways and there are even stories that on certain nights, ghostly dancers can be seen whirling around in the ballroom.

Early this century, a well-known local poacher called Jim Mace crept into Breckles Hall in the hope of shooting some partridges. Jim and his friend knew of the supernatural stories but hardly gave them a second thought as they filled their bags with birds. Then they saw a coach draw up outside the hall and a beautiful woman covered in jewels step out, ready for the ball.

In that instance she looked straight into Jim Mace's eyes and he fell to the ground with a terrible scream. His friend rushed to get help but no one would return with him to the hall after they heard his story. It wasn't until the next day that the parish vicar found Jim Mace's body and noted how his face was frozen in fear.

28. The Ghost of a Frozen Chicken

A ghost — sad, bizarre, and deserving a place in the annals of commercial food-preparation — is associated with Pond Square in London's Highgate. It is the ghost of a half-naked, half-frozen chicken.

The ghost maker in this tale is no less a philosopher than the great Francis Bacon, once Lord Chancellor of England. In 1626, though, when he was 65 years old, he had been convicted of bribery, sentenced to the Tower of London, and fined 40,000 pounds. Although pardoned later, Bacon was forbidden to hold public office again.

Thus freed from the struggle for worldly powers, he turned his mind to the mysteries of the universe and to the methods by which a man might solve them.

He was riding through the streets of Highgate one snowy March day in 1626 when a universal mystery occurred to him. Why was grass that had lain under snow all winter still green and fresh when his carriage wheels exposed it to the air? Did the snow somehow act as a preservative?

Bacon instantly stopped his carriage at Pond Square and ordered his coachman to buy a chicken from a farm nearby. Next, he had the coachman kill the bird, pluck off most of its feathers, and clean out the abdominal cavity. Then, to the amazement of the small crowd pressing around him, Bacon stooped down and began stuffing the bird with snow. This done, he put it in a sack and filled the sack with more snow.

While he was treating the chicken in this unnatural way, a fit of shivering seized him, and he collapsed on the snow. He was taken to the home of his friend Lord Arundel, and died there within a few days.

What happened to Lord Bacon after he died, nobody knows, but the chicken, bound, it seems, to the environs of Pond Square by the sudden outrage that befell it, has been frequently seen there since its death. Stripped of its feathers and shivering, it invariably half runs, and half flaps, always in circles. "It was a big, whitish bird," according to Mrs. John Greenhill, who resided at Pond Square during World War II and often saw the chicken on moonlit nights. Aircraftman Terence Long was another witness, also during the war, who was crossing the square one night when he heard the sound of hooves and carriage wheels. He looked around but saw nothing — except a shivering, half-naked chicken flapping pathetically in circles. An Air Raid Precautions fire-watcher came along and told Aircraftman Long that the bird was a habitué of the square. A man had tried to snare it a month or two earlier, he said, but it had disappeared into a brick wall.

One January night in 1969, a motorist who was delayed in Pond Square with car trouble noticed a large white bird near a wall. Seeing that most of its feathers had been plucked, and thinking that a gang of youths might have abused the bird, he looked about him before going to rescue the poor creature. When he turned back, the bird was gone. A year later in February, a young man and woman were saying good night to each other when a big white bird alighted noiselessly on the ground beside them. It ran twice in a circle and then vanished into the darkness.

29. Novak's Mischievous Ghost

Movie actress Kim Novak believes she lived in a haunted castle in 1964 during the filming of *The Amorous Adventures of Moll Flanders.* Exteriors for the movie were filmed in England, and Miss Novak lived in Chilbam Castle, Chilbam village, Kent, during her visit.

One evening, after taking a bath, she went to sleep. She woke up suddenly and was mystified to discover that the bathtub had been refilled again — at the precise temperature the actress prefers for her bathing water!

On another occasion, a bouquet of flowers was sent to the actress by an admirer. The bouquet vanished mysteriously during the night while Miss Novak was sleeping and was discovered downstairs in the morning.

The mischievous pranks directed at Miss Novak are just one of a series of ghostly manifestations linked to English castles.

30. The Vanishing Nun

Residents of Evansville, Indiana, have been mystified in recent years by the occasional manifestation of what is called "the vanishing nun."

On one occasion, several teenagers were playing baseball at a neighbourhood lot. The black-clad nun approached, stood quietly, and watched their game. During a heated dispute, the boys turned toward the nun.

"Was it a foul ball or not, sister?" a youth inquired. Suddenly, without warning, the nun vanished!

At other times, the "vanishing nun" has been seen by reputable citizens who meet her walking along the street. "She has been here for many years," a woman wrote. "My mother can recall stories of her appearance in the nineteen thirties."

Appearances of the "vanishing nun" are reported in the Evansville newspapers. However, no one has ventured an explanation into the origin of the apparition.

31. The Lady of Glamis

In 1540, the wife of the sixth Lord Glamis was burnt as a witch. Today, her ghost haunts Glamis Castle in Scotland, where she has been seen by the Queen Mother, amongst others.

32. The Faceless Miner

Stephen Dimbleby was a miner at Silverwood Colliery, South Yorkshire. One evening in 1982, his colleagues were alarmed to see him rush out of the mine, screaming and crying, into the arms of an amazed pit deputy.

Later, Dimbleby recovered sufficiently to relate what had happened. He had been walking towards the coal seam to start his shift when he saw a shadowy figure ahead of him. At first he thought it was one of his colleagues — and then he realised there should not have been anyone else in that part of the mine at that time of night.

The figure was wearing a waistcoat and a grubby shirt and had an old-fashioned square helmet with a light on it. The young miner lifted his lamp to get a better look at the man, and then froze in his tracks — the figure had no face!

The pit deputy later revealed that several other miners had reported similar strange sightings in the same area. Coal Board officials then confirmed that a miner had been killed at that spot in 1968, when he was trapped in a coal-cutting machine. At that time, miners wore exactly the type of clothing that Stephen Dimbleby had so vividly described!

33. A Headless Ghost

The ghost of King Charles I of England, who was beheaded in 1649, has often been seen standing by a table in the library at Windsor Castle in Berkshire. The headless ghost has also been seen at Maple Hall in Cheshire, England.

34. A Phantom Car

In the early 1960s, a car plunged into the Kyle of Lochalsh, Scotland, and its occupants were drowned. The car was identical to a phantom car that had been sighted regularly in the region for over 20 years. After the accident, the ghost vehicle was never seen again.

35. Incomplete Symphonies

Rosemary Brown, a London widow, owned a piano but was not very accomplished at playing it. She knew only one musician — a former church organist who was trying to teach her to play. The music world and the rest of London was hard-pressed to explain then, how, in 1964, she began writing pieces of music that seemed to come from the masters themselves.

Indeed, Brown was a self-proclaimed clairvoyant, whose mother and grandmother were also alleged to be psychic. She said that Franz Liszt, who had "visited" her once before in a vision when she was a child, appeared to her again and began bringing music from the likes of Beethoven, Bach, Chopin and others. Each dictated his own music. Sometimes, she said, they controlled her hands, moving them to the proper keys; sometimes they only dictated the notes. But among the works she produced were the completion of Beethoven's *Tenth* and *Eleventh Symphonies*, which had been incomplete at the time of his death; a forty-page sonata by Schubert and numerous works by Liszt and the others.

Musicians and psychologists examined the material and investigated every line of music and every line of Brown's testimony. Although some music critics dismissed the work as copied, and not copied well, others were amazed at the quality of the work. All agree that each piece she produced was definitely written in the style of the composer to which it was attributed. No one has found evidence that she was lying, and most investigators pronounced her to be sincere. Quality music or not, it was music well beyond Brown's capability.

Liszt, however, had failed Brown in one respect. In his first visit to her, the clairvoyant claimed, Liszt had promised to make her a great musician one day, yet she remained an unaccomplished pianist. Perhaps that is why, as Mrs. Brown's story goes, the composers, who dictated to her in English would often raise their hands and yell "Mein Gott!"

36. Came Back for his Dog

Joe Benson of Wendover, Utah, was a spiritual leader of the Goshute Indians. His constant companion was a magnificent German shepherd he called Sky.

As Benson grew old and his vision failed, Sky guarded his steps and kept him from harm. Benson's health continued to decline and one day in late 1962, he told his wife Mabel that he was about to die. She notified the relatives and soon they and their children had come to his bedside. But, because they no longer followed the Indian traditions, they insisted that he be taken to the hospital in nearby Owyhee, Nevada. They ignored his protests and Sky's deep-throated growls, and carried him away.

Benson stayed at the hospital for only a short time. When the doctors saw there was nothing to be done, they sent him back home, where soon afterwards, in January 1963, he died.

After the funeral ceremonies, several of the mourners asked if they could have Sky. Mrs. Benson, who saw that the dog seemed to be grieving even more than she was, sensed that this would be wrong, so she kept him. Ten days later, she happened to look out of the window to see someone coming up the road to the house. She built a fire in the cookstove and put on some fresh coffee. When she looked up, she saw someone she recognised in the doorway — her late husband.

True to her people's traditions, she gently told him he was dead and had no business in this world. Joe Benson nodded and only said, "I am going. I came back for my dog."

He whistled and Sky, his tail wagging furiously, came running into the kitchen.

"I want his leash," Benson said. His wife took it down from a hook on the wall and handed it to him, taking care not to touch him. He snapped the leash on Sky's collar and the old man and his dog went out of the door, down the steps, and on to the path that wound around the hill.

After hesitating for a few moments, Mrs. Benson ran outside to the other side of the hill. Joe and Sky were nowhere to be seen.

As it happened, Joe and Mabel's next-door neighbour, their daughter Arvilla Benson Urban, witnessed this strange visitation and swore to it in an affidavit. She said, "I saw my father enter the house and not more than a few minutes later I saw him leave with his dog on a leash. I saw my mother go after him and I, after I could think, went after her. "When I reached the top of the hill, my father and his dog were gone."

For the next several days, the young men of the family searched for the dog without success. It appeared that Sky had vanished, with his beloved master, into another world.

37. Recording a Ghostly Song

In 1905, a lady singer whose career had not been very successful decided to kill herself. She climbed on to the roof of a theatre in Clapham, London, and started to sing dramatically. Then she fell through the skylight, to her death. She has been seen in the theatre several times since, and her plaintive song has even been recorded on tape.

38. The Ghostly Appearances

Captain Robert Loft and Second Officer Don Repo died when their Eastern Airlines L-1011 TriStar crashed in Southern Florida on December 29, 1972. But their ghosts were seen for quite some time afterwards. The first sighting was made by one of the airline's vice-presidents. He was chatting to a uniformed pilot on a flight to San Francisco when he suddenly realised he was talking to Captain Loft. The figure then vanished.

In February 1974, on a flight to Mexico City, a stewardess saw Don Repo. She mentioned this to the flight engineer who said that he too, had seen him. He said Repo had warned him to watch out for fire on the plane. Sure enough, when the plane took off from Mexico City, one of the engines burst into flames. Fortunately, the fire was quickly put out.

The two men were sighted on several other flights during 1974 but have not been seen since.

39. Strange Events in Gloucester Jail

In 1969, Robert Gore, a prisoner at Gloucester Jail, England, was so bored at Christmas that he decided to play with a glass tumbler and some letters spread over a table.

Much to his surprise, the glass suddenly began moving of its own accord. The glass moved to several of the letters in turn and spelled out the name of Jenny Godfrey. She had been murdered at that spot in the 15th century by a drunken man. The spirit of Jenny then spelled out to the prisoners several predictions of events that were about to happen. At first the prisoners scoffed, but later, when some of the predictions came true, they began to believe in the power of their spiritual contact.

There were also instances of clothes and other objects being thrown around the cells at the jail. On one occasion, one of the prisoners reported seeing a ghostly hand in his cell. Eventually, Jenny's spirit appeared less and less but to this day, strange events occur in Gloucester Jail.

40. A Cavalier's Ghost

During the English Civil War (1642-49), the Royalists (supporters of King Charles I) had to meet in secret. One group of Royalists used to meet in the cellar of the Ring O' Bells public house at Middleton, near Manchester. They were safe there until one day someone betrayed their hiding place to the enemy, the Roundheads.

One of the men in the cellar that day was the son of Lord Stannycliffe of Stannycliffe Hall, near Middleton. He managed to get away from the cellar and made his escape through a secret passage that led to the parish church. But the Roundheads knew about the passage and the young man was caught and killed.

Stannycliffe's body was buried under the flagstones in the cellar of the public house where he and his friends used to meet. And to this day, he haunts the Ring O' Bells. He has been seen on several occasions, weeping and wandering through the passageways of the building.

Even people who know nothing of the story of this ghost have reported strange events whilst visiting the Ring O' Bells. Customers have mentioned going to the bar to buy a drink, only to be pushed away by someone or something that was not there, and the owners have often heard the sound of ghostly footsteps in the passageways.

At one time it was suggested that the cavalier's remains be removed from beneath the cellar floor and given a proper burial. But it was decided that as the ghost did no harm, it should be allowed to remain in the building.

If you go to the Ring O' Bells today, you will find that there is still a 'cavalier's seat' in the bar and a table known as the 'ghosts table', at which Royalist ghosts are said to sit.

41. Saved by a Ghostly Comrade

British soldier Gerald Pooler owed his life to a ghostly comrade. Corporal Pooler had left his London home to serve in the Royal Signals Regiment during the Burma campaign of World War Two.

One night, he took cover behind a pagoda during a Japanese artillery bombardment. He had decided to get some sleep when a shadow fell across him. He looked up to see a Sikh soldier, who told him that his captain wanted him at once.

When he arrived at the Signals office, he was told nobody had called him. Puzzled, he headed back to the pagoda — and found that its top had been hit by a shell. A chunk of stone weighing a ton was lying on the spot where he had been napping!

Pooler said later: "The astonishing thing was that there were no Sikh soldiers at our HQ. The nearest were 20 miles away."

42. A Lovers Ghost

Deep moans, flying furniture, and shrill screams of deathly agony are manifestations of the ghost of Sarah Taylor in a famous mansion in Washington, D.C. "The Octagon," as the brick mansion was named upon completion in 1800, is an important historical shrine and the present headquarters of the American Institute of Architects.

Colonel John Taylor, his wife, and their attractive daughter occupied the mansion for many years. Legend says Sarah Taylor fell in love with a handsome young naval officer. She was preparing for her wedding when her fiancé was killed on the night that the British forces burnt the White House during the war of 1812.

The young bride-to-be never recovered from the shock of her lover's death. She stayed in her bedroom, ate sparingly, and spent her years in mourning. She never ventured outside the mansion. Distraught and overwhelmed by her unnatural grief, the young girl leaped down the stairways one night. Her frail body was crushed by the fall.

In the 150 years since her death, the grieving ghost of "Suicide Sarah" has prowled through the ancient mansion. "I liked the job, but I quit," a former janitor told a journalist recently. "Footsteps followed me up the stairway. I would turn around quickly, but there was no one behind me. At night, I heard screams that sounded like a dying woman, coming from the foot of the stairway."

Another maintenance man verified these reports. "Her ghost used to shift furniture around the room," he blurted. "I saw a chair fly through the air one night. There were cold spots in some of the rooms."

Several years ago, every bell and clock in the mansion would ring at certain hours of the night. Some say it is "Suicide Sarah" tolling for the spirit of her dead lover.

43. Kidd's Return

Captain William Kidd, the British sea captain whose piracy in the Indian Ocean made him notorious, was hanged at Wapping, London in 1701, ostensibly for killing one of his crew.

His corpse was left strung up long enough for three tides to wash over it.

Days later, a shadowy figure was seen emerging from the water of the old Execution Dock. In recent years, the same figure, believed to be Kidd, has been reported at Wapping Old Stairs.

44. Visitation from a Dead Husband

Mrs. Mary Travers put aside her book when she heard a taxi halt in front of her home in Sudbury, Ontario, Canada, on the night of January 21, 1910. Her husband, George, was an insurance salesman. He had been away on a prolonged sales trip, and his familiar footsteps on the porch were a welcome sound.

Mrs. Travers hurried to the front hallway and unlocked the front door. Her husband stomped the snow from his feet and entered the house silently, his hat pulled low over his eyes.

"Welcome home," Mrs. Travers smiled.

Her husband stood quietly with his back to his wife. Mrs. Travers was puzzled by this unusual behaviour. "George, are you sick?" she inquired.

The figure turned slowly to face the woman. Mrs. Travers screamed with shocked horror. The face staring at her was undoubtedly her husband — but it was a terrifying, chalk-white death mask!

The woman's anguished screams brought neighbours dashing to her home. The mysterious figure had vanished. The shrill ring of the telephone interrupted their efforts to calm the hysterical woman, who babbled her frightening story.

A neighbour answered the phone. "Train No. 17 plunged off a bridge into the Spanish River tonight," a railroad official said. "It is my duty to inform the family that George Travers was one of the passengers who was killed."

The eerie visitation from a dead husband was verified by several neighbours who heard Mrs.Travers's story before news of her husband's death was announced by the railroad. Elderly residents in Sudbury can still recall the chilling incident — and wonder!

45. A Crying Ghost

Among Gaelic people, banshees — female guardian spirits — have been well known for centuries. A banshee will attach herself to a person or family, watch over them during their life, and foretell an imminent death by shrieking, crying, and wailing. Such is the case with the Rossmore banshee of County Monaghan, Ireland.

Her terrible wailing was first heard in 1801, when Gen. Robert Cunningham, the first Baron Rossmore, lay dying. William Rossmore, the sixth baron, described the original appearance of the banshee, a story passed down through the family over the years:

"Robert Rossmore was on terms of great friendship with Sir Jonah and Lady Barrington, and once when they met at a Dublin drawing-room, Rossmore persuaded the Barringtons to come over the next day to Mount Kennedy, where he was then living. As the invited guests proposed to rise early, they retired to bed in good time, and slept soundly until two o'clock in the morning, when Sir Jonah was awakened by a wild and plaintive cry. He lost no time in rousing his wife, and the scared couple got up and opened the window, which looked over the grass plot beneath.

It was a moonlight night and the objects around the house were easily discernible, but there was nothing to be seen in the direction from where the eerie sounds came.

Now thoroughly frightened, Lady Barrington called her maid, who just would not listen or look, but fled in terror to the servants' quarters. The uncanny noise continued for about half and hour when it suddenly ceased. All at once a weird cry, 'Rossmore, Rossmore, Rossmore' was heard, and then all was still."

The Barringtons looked at each other in dismay, and were utterly bewildered as to what the cry could mean. They decided, however, not to mention the incident at Mount Kennedy, and returned to bed in the hope of resuming their broken slumbers.

They were not left long undisturbed, for at seven o'clock, they were awakened by a loud knocking at the bedroom door, and Sir Jonah's servant, Layer, entered the room, his face white with terror.

"What's the matter, what's the matter?" asked Sir Jonah. "Is anyone dead?"

"Oh sir," answered the man, "Lord Rossmore's footman has just gone by in great haste. He told me that the lord, after coming from the castle, had gone to bed in perfect health but that about half past two this morning, his own man on hearing a noise in his master's room went to him, and found him in the agonies of death, and before he could alarm the servants, his lordship was dead."

Shrieking and wailing and crying, 'Rossmore, Rossmore,' the banshee has announced the death of every Rossmore heir since then, including that of the sixth baron, who died in 1958.

46. Writing on a Blackboard

In 1828, a British ship out of Liverpool, England, was heading due west towards Nova Scotia in the icy waters of the North Atlantic. The ship had been at sea for many weeks when one day the first mate, Robert Bruce, found a strange man writing on a blackboard in the captain's cabin. Bruce was astonished to discover someone he did not recognise on board and, mystified, went to report the event to the captain. The captain was incredulous. How could there be anyone on the ship whom neither he nor the mate had seen before?

Nonetheless, he followed Bruce to the cabin and looked at the blackboard. The words "STEER TO THE NOR'WEST," were clearly written for all to see. The stranger, however, had disappeared. The captain asked everyone on the ship to write the same words on a slate, but nobody's handwriting matched that on the blackboard.

The captain was now altogether at a loss to explain the apparition and its message, but he ordered the ship's course be changed to northwest. Some hours later, the ship's lookout sighted another vessel stuck fast in ice. All her passengers were taken on board, and among them Bruce recognised the man he had seen in the cabin. The captain then asked him to write down the words "STEER TO THE NOR'WEST"; his handwriting matched that of the original message, exactly!

According to the captain of the icebound vessel, the passenger concerned had fallen asleep at about the same time that his double was seen; when he awoke, he had announced with complete certainty that they would all be saved.

47. Herne, the Hunter

For over 250 years, people have reported seeing the ghost of a man wearing antlers on his head in the Great Park at Windsor in Berkshire, England. He is Herne, the hunter, who hanged himself in the park.

48. The Last of the Darrell Family

Littlecote Manor in Wiltshire, southern England, was built between 1490 and 1520. It is a beautiful house in luscious surroundings — but it is also haunted.

One night in 1575, Mother Barnes, a midwife, was brought secretly to the house from the nearby village of Great Shefford to deliver a baby girl. The father, 'Wild' Darrell, the last of the Darrell family, took the baby and threw her into the fire!

Darrell himself lived until 1598, when he was killed while hunting in the park at a place still known as Darrells's Style.

The ghosts of 'Wild' Darrell and his hounds still haunt the park, and the room where the baby was killed is frequently visited by the ghosts of Mother Barnes, the baby and her mother.

49. The Dog-like Skeleton

For one glorious year, Edward Cranswell was very pleased with his new house, Croglin Hall, in England. But he changed his mind during the summer of 1875. His sister, Amelia, was unable to sleep one night and was sitting gazing out at the garden. As she watched, a strange dog-like skeleton came across the lawn and began scratching at the window.

Amelia screamed with terror and ran to the door. But it was locked. In her panic she dropped the key and could not find it in the dark. She could hear her two brothers pounding on her door but by now, the skeleton had removed a pane of glass. A bony arm came through the broken pane and began to open the window.

When her brothers eventually managed to open the door, they found Amelia unconscious on the floor. Blood was pouring from terrible wounds on her throat, face and shoulders. Her brother, Michael, saw the skeleton running away.

After a long convalescence in Switzerland, Amelia returned to Croglin Hall in spite of her brothers' misgivings. For, during her absence, there had been other reports in the area of girls being attacked by a strange creature.

It was not long after that the skeleton appeared once again at Croglin. But this time, Amelia's brothers were prepared. They now slept near to Amelia's bedroom and ruled that none of doors were to be locked. When they heard Amelia's terrified screams, Michael dashed to her room and Edward headed for the front door. The skeleton ran away towards the churchyard. As it scrambled over the churchyard wall, Edward fired his pistol. The creature staggered for a moment and then slowly began to make its way to the family vault of the Fishers — the family who had owned Croglin before the Cranswells.

Next day, the brothers took some local men and broke into the vault. Every coffin was broken and pieces were strewn across the floor. Only one coffin was intact. They opened the coffin and found a shrivelled, dog-like creature inside. It had a flesh wound in its leg! The villagers agreed that the corpse should be burnt. The terror of Croglin Hall was never seen again.

50. Child of the Occult World

Swirling snow drifts covered the streets of Philadelphia when a blizzard descended on the city on December 4, 1890. Dr. S. Weir Mitchell, one of the nation's most skilful neurologists, had endured a tiring day with his patients. The trip home had been even more tiring, and quite fatigued, the good doctor prepared for bed.

He was barely under the warm covers when his doorbell pealed sharply. He mumbled as he padded across the living room and opened the door. A small, frail child was standing in the swirling snow. She was clad in a thin, cheap dress, and her shoulders shivered under a ragged shawl.

"My mother is very ill," she pleaded above the howl of the blizzard. "Won't you please come and treat her?"

"I've already gone to bed, dear," Dr. Mitchell answered. "There are several other doctors who maintain night hours."

The girl raised her pale, drawn face and looked directly at Dr. Mitchell, "You, sir, are the one who can make my mother well."

There was something pathetic about the young child, and Dr. Mitchell agreed to accompany her. He dressed quickly, pulled on his thick overcoat, and followed the pale child through the roaring blizzard. The girl was strangely silent throughout their journey to a shabby tenement. The doctor was led upstairs to an apartment.

"Mother is in there and needs you very much," the girl said, pointing to a room leading from the dim hallway. Dr. Mitchell found a woman lying in the chilled darkness. She was suffering from pneumonia. The woman had been a servant in the doctor's home for a few months some years ago.

Dr. Mitchell spent the next 30 minutes administering to the needs of his patient. When his treatment was completed, the doctor snapped the lock on his medical bag.

"You are a very lucky woman," he informed the patient. "You would have been dead by morning if you daughter had not insisted that I make this call."

A bewildered look covered the woman's face. "You must be mistaken, doctor. My daughter died over a year ago!"

"Impossible! Who was the girl who led me to your bedside?" Dr. Mitchell was equally puzzled. He described the girl, her appearance, and her clothing.

"Doctor, those clothes are in that cupboard," said the ailing woman. She feebly rose and pointed to a small cupboard.

Dr. Mitchell flung open the doors of the cupboard. There was the same cheap, worn dress. The identical ragged shawl was hanging limply on a hook. Incredibly, the clothes were warm as if they had just been worn. Yet they could not possibly have been out on that blizzardly night!

"Those were my little girl's favourite clothes," said the patient. "We bought a nice white dress for her burial!"

Dr. Mitchell told the story many times over the years. Since the famed physician was president of the American Association of Physicians, president of the American Neurological Association, and the recipient of degrees from several universities, there were few who dared to call him a "crackpot!" He had had a strange encounter with an eerie child of the occult world.

51. The Ghost of Washington Irving

Would the author of one of the most famous American ghost stories ever return from dead to play a prank? Washington Irving, author of *The Legend of Sleepy Hollow*, was a witty man who liked to have fun, sometimes at the expense of others. Shortly after Irving's death, one of the author's old friends, a Dr. J.G. Cogswell, was working in the library when he saw a man shelve a book and disappear. Cogswell felt certain the man was Irving — until he saw another ghostly figure, the image of a second deceased friend, return a book as well.

That was not the end of it. Irving's nephew, Pierre, reportedly saw the ghost of his uncle in the Irving home in Tarrytown, New York. He and his two daughters said they clearly saw the famed author walk through the parlour and into the library, where he used to do his work.

While alive, Irving professed no belief in ghosts. The headless horseman of his writing, after all, was really a mortal dressed to scare away a rival. It is likely his nephew shared that belief — until Irving himself proved them both wrong.

52. An Enormous Black Dog

An enormous black dog is said to haunt Gatcombe, the home of Princess Anne. The dog is thought to be the black hound of Odin, a Viking warrior who plundered the area 1000 years ago.

53. An Apparition that Saved the Ship

In the early years of this century, a sailor on *HMS Society* was drowned. A few nights later, the captain was woken up by the sailor's ghost. 'Cast the lead, sir!' said the apparition. Then it vanished.

The captain did as he had been instructed, and found that his ship was off course and sailing in only 10 metres (36 feet) of water. The ghost had prevented the ship from running aground.

54. A Ghost with a Message

Early in the morning of December 6, 1955, Lucian Landau, a London businessman, had an unusual dream. He was sleeping in the home of Constantine Antoniades in Geneva when he felt someone entering his room. When he turned over in bed, he saw a faint pool of light in which he gradually perceived the figure of his host's late wife. Next to her figure stood an Alsatian dog with an unusual brown coat. The apparition soon began to disappear, but while dissolving, Landau heard it say, "Tell him."

The London businessman didn't hesitate to impart the information to his host when they met later in the day. But he didn't explain exactly what had occurred. Instead, he merely asked whether his host's wife had ever had an Alsatian dog.

"Oh, yes," responded Mr. Antoniades. "He is still alive."

This response puzzled Landau, since there was no evidence of a dog in the house. Antoniades then explained that he boarded the dog at a kennel when his wife became ill, since he couldn't look after it.

When Landau finally told his host about the ghostly visitation, Antoniades called the kennel, only to learn that the dog had been destroyed a few days earlier.

The words "Tell him" were finally beginning to make sense.

When an investigator from the Society for Psychical Research in Great Britain looked into the case, Antoniades corroborated the remarkable episode. "I affirm," he testified, "that there was not any photograph of my wife with the dog or the dog alone anywhere in the house where Landau could have seen it before the incident occurred."

55. The Notification of Death

World War I ended officially at 11 a.m. on November 11, 1918. On that day, Harold Owen was an officer on the *HMS Astraea*, a British cruiser then anchored in Table Bay, Union of South Africa. To celebrate the armistice, the ship's captain invited all the officers for drinks in his cabin, but Owen, then 21 years old, was unable to enter into the happy mood. A feeling of apprehension gripped him, 'Had his brother, Wilfred, survived the war?' A fit of the deepest depression settled on him. Before long, the *Astraea* left Table Bay for the coast of Cameroon. While anchored off Victoria, Own fell ill with malaria and, in a weakened and still depressed state, had "an extraordinary and inexplicable experience," which he later described:

"I had gone down to my cabin thinking of writing some letters. I drew aside the door curtain and stepped inside and to my amazement, I saw Wilfred sitting in my chair. I felt a shock run through me with appalling force and with it I could feel the blood draining away from my face. I did not rush towards him but walked jerkily into the cabin — all my limbs stiff and slow to respond. I did not sit down but looking at him I spoke quietly: 'Wilfred, how did you get here?' He did not rise and I saw that he was involuntarily immobile, but his eyes, which had never left mine, were alive with the familiar look of trying to make me understand. When I spoke his whole face broke into his sweetest and most endearing dark smile. I felt no fear — I had not when I first drew my door curtain and saw him there, only an exquisite mental pleasure at thus beholding him. All I was conscious of was a sensation of enormous shock and profound astonishment that he should be there in my cabin. I spoke again: "Wilfred dear, how can you be here, it's just not possible . . ." He did not speak but only smiled his most gentle smile.

This 'not speaking' did not seem strange or even unnatural now as it had done at first. It was not only in some inexplicable way perfectly natural but even radiated a quality which made his presence with me undeniably right and in no way out of the ordinary. I loved having him there; I could not, and did not want to try to understand how he had got there. I was content to accept the fact that he was there with me. I could not question anything, the meeting in itself was complete and strangely perfect.

He was in uniform and I remember thinking how out of place the *khaki* looked amongst the cabin furnishings. With this thought I must have turned my eyes away from him for when I looked back, my cabin chair was empty!

I felt the blood run slowly back to my face and looseness into my limbs and with this, an overpowering sense of emptiness and absolute loss. I wondered if I had been dreaming but looking down I saw that I was still standing.

Suddenly I felt terribly tired and moving to my bunk, I lay down; instantly I went into a deep oblivious sleep. When

I woke up I knew with absolute certainty that Wilfred was dead."

Wilfred Owen, the famous war poet, was killed on November 4, 1918. His parents received notification of his death at 12 noon on November 11, one hour after the hostilities had ceased. He is perhaps best remembered for his poem *Strange Meeting*, in which he imagined an encounter with the spirits of those who had died in the war.

56. Where Did the Oil Come From?

In early August 1919, oil began to "spurt" from the walls and ceilings of Swanton Novers Rectory in Norfolk, England. At first it was supposed that the house stood over a natural oil well and that the liquid was being soaked up by the walls and then somehow ejected. But when the oil was found to be refined gasoline, this theory was abandoned. Showers of water, methylated spirits, and sandalwood oil followed. At one point, the oil flow was at the rate of a quart every 10 minutes. The rector, Rev. Hugh Guy, was soon obliged to move his furnishings into another house.

A magician and his wife, a Mr. and Mrs. Oswald Williams, went to the rectory to investigate. Putting pails of salted water about, they hid and watched. On September 9, they announced that the culprit was the 15-year-old scullery maid, whom they caught throwing salt water on the ceiling. But the girl denied it and said she had been beaten to make her confess.

The foreman of an oil company went to check the house and caught two gallons of oil in four hours. And a second magician-turned-investigator stated that he observed the flow of "barrels" of oil during his visit to the premises. The source of the oil was never determined, but it seemed unlikely that the girl could have handled such copious quantities of it.

57. The Lieutenant's Ghost

On January 21, 1918, three officers were standing on the bridge of the German submarine *U-65* when they spotted a man standing near the bows. Where he had come from they could not imagine, for the submarine had only just surfaced.

The officers shouted to the man, but when he turned to look up at the bridge, the three officers received a shock — glaring at them was Lieutenant Forster, who had been killed a few months before. The ghost stared at the men for a minute or so, then vanished as suddenly as it had appeared.

58. The Vanishing Girl

On July 13, 1974, Maurice Goodenough was driving up Bluebell Hill in Kent, southern England, when suddenly, the figure of a young girl appeared in his headlights. He braked as hard as he could, but he was not quick enough and the car hit the girl. Goodenough jumped out of the car and ran over to where she was lying. She had serious head injuries, so he carried her to the roadside and covered her with a blanket before driving to the police station.

The police dashed to the scene of the accident, but when they arrived, all they found was the blanket. The girl had vanished. Tracker dogs were used to find her, but without success.

Later, the driver discovered that other drivers had seen the girl on other occasions. Some had even given her a ride, but each time, she had vanished. Apparently, two girls had been killed at that spot in 1967. Perhaps one of them had come back as a ghost to haunt the living!

59. The Ghost Bird

A group of men were standing near the lodge of the legal offices at Lincoln's Inn, London on the evening of February 25, 1913, when they heard a terrified scream. They looked up and saw, silhouetted in a window, the figure of a man fighting off an invisible assailant.

They rushed up the stairs to the first floor office but they were too late — Charles Appleby, a young barrister, lay dead on the floor, covered in blood.

In the months that followed, a number of other tenants occupied the offices, but they all left because of the evil atmosphere that was present. A short while later, another barrister, John Radlett, was found hanged in the same office where Charles Appleby had been found. There were deep scratches on the inside of his locked door; they looked as if they had been made by the claws of an enormous bird.

When stories began to circulate about the ghost bird that haunted the offices in Lincoln's Inn, two newspaper editors, Sir Max Pemberton and Ralph Blumenfeld, decided to investigate. They locked themselves in the ill-famed room, sprinkled powdered French chalk all over the floor, and began their vigil.

The two men spent the evening playing cards, and by midnight, they were getting bored with the whole idea. It seemed obvious that nothing untoward was going to happen. They were about to leave, when the locked door swung open. The windows, which had been bolted, opened by themselves, and a harsh wind entered the room, extinguishing the gaslight.

There was a horrific beating noise, which sounded like the flapping of enormous wings. In the dim light the two men could just see a large, dark object moving across the room and out through a wall. Then the noise stopped, and the light came on again.

A reporter, who had been waiting downstairs, heard the commotion, rushed into the room, and all three men stared in disbelief at the floor. In the chalk, running from the centre of the room to the corner, was a set of gigantic claw marks!

A few years later, the building was demolished and the giant bird, if that is what it was, was never heard of again.

60. A Dramatic Ghost

During the performance of a play presented at a theatre in Wellington, Surrey, in 1973, many people in the audience were puzzled as to why one actor had remained in the shadows during the performance and had taken no active part in the play.

This puzzled the producer even more, for he had not cast any such actor in his play. Furthermore, the doorway where people saw the man standing, did not even exist!

The ghost appeared on subsequent evenings, and twenty-four people from four performances said they saw him. Everyone who described him said he was dressed in 16th century clothing. But who the man was, and why he wanted to take part in the performance, remains a mystery.

61. White Lady of the Lake

A young couple was parked on a lonely lovers' lane outside of White Lake Rock, Texas, on the evening of March 13, 1968. Locked in a tight embrace, they were oblivious of their dark surroundings. Suddenly, the dark night was illuminated by a dancing glob of white light in the distance.

"It's probably a police patrol," Robert Johnson advised his date. The young couple watched the fuzzy white light move closer to their parked car. "That's no police car," said the girl. "The light is all fuzzy."

The unusual light glided down the country lane and was transformed into a gaunt, ghastly woman. Her ragged garments were dripping wet. A bony hand reached for the door handle of the automobile.

"I was almost paralysed with fear, but moved quickly enough to snap the door button lock," Johnson recalled. "I barely heard my date pleading with me to get the car started. I was almost hypnotised by the ugliness of the hag's face."

Johnson started his engine, floored the gas pedal, and left the horrible ghoul standing in the darkness. "When I looked back, she had disappeared," he said. "I thought it was a prank and turned around and went back. The white lady was gone, and there was just a puddle of water where she had been standing. There were water stains on the door of my car."

The strange "White Lady of the Lake" is no figment of young lover' imaginations. She is frequently observed by people driving in the area of White Rock Lake. She delights in frightening young lovers parked along the lonely roads.

"An old story says a woman drowned herself when her fiancé left her standing at the church steps on their wedding day," a resident of the area said. "Perhaps her ghost is jealous and delights in frightening people in love." The spectral apparition has been reported for several years — a strange figure gliding through the night, dripping with lake water.

62. Sir George and Lady Tyron

On June 22, 1893, a number of guests gathered for tea at the London home of Vice-Admiral Sir George and Lady Tyron. When the admiral, in full dress uniform, walked down the stairs and out of the door, his wife screamed in horror. The guests were also surprised, for they knew that the admiral was not even in London at the time.

He was miles away, on board his ship *Victoria*, off the coast of Tripoli. What none of them could possibly realise was that at that very moment the *Victoria* was going down with over half its officers and men.

Sir George was among the many that perished.

63. A Psychic Experience

Sometimes a psychic experience will take the edge off an otherwise shattering tragedy. When nineteen-year-old Wendy Finkel was killed in a car accident near Point Mugu in the southern California coast, her mother didn't need to hear about it from the police. She already knew. The date was Thursday, November 19, 1987.

It was the day before Wendy's birthday. The college student and three of her friends had driven in from Santa Barbara to take someone to the Los Angeles airport. Two of the students planned to attend a rock concert. They took Wendy out for dinner and dancing, and then visited her sister, who lived near the University of California at Los Angeles. The Finkels were looking forward to Wendy's birthday that Friday and especially to having their children home for Thanksgiving. The tragedy struck sometime early in the morning, when the car carrying the students apparently drove off the Pacific Coast Highway, and plunged down the embankment into the sea. A fisherman happened to see the 1986 Honda Civic floating in the water upside down the next morning, and the bodies of Wendy's three friends were soon recovered.

At the same time as the accident, Mrs. Finkel had awakened suddenly in her Woodland Hills home, gasping for air. "I felt like I was drowning," she later told reporters. "I couldn't get any air in my lungs. I looked at the clock and it said two something. I'm assuming that's when the car got to Point Mugu and went off the cliff."

Wendy's body was never recovered, though her mother has little doubt about her fate.

64. A Tragedy-struck Oil Tanker

Tragedy struck the oil tanker *SS Watertown* when it sailed from New York City to the Panama Canal early in December 1924. Two seamen, James Courtney and Michael Meehan, were cleaning a cargo tank when they were accidentally killed by gas fumes. Their bodies were buried at sea in proper maritime tradition on December 4.

The ghosts of the *SS Watertown* appeared the next day, but not in the form of sheet-clad phantoms stalking the ship's decks. The faces of the two unfortunate men were seen following the ship in the water. The disconcerting phantoms seen day after day by the ship's captain, Keith Tracy, and by the entire crew, seemed determined to follow the ship right through the canal.

Captain Tracy reported these eerie events to his head office when the ship docked in New Orleans, and officials from the company suggested that he try photographing them. He eventually delivered a roll of film with six exposures to the Cities Service Company, which had it commercially developed. While five of the shots ravelled nothing unusual, the sixth exposure clearly showed the two faces lugubriously following the ship.

Interestingly enough, the Cities Service Company didn't try to play down the fascinating story or hide it from the public. They reported it openly in their own company magazine, *Service*, in 1934, and even displayed a blow-up of the photograph in the main lobby of the Cities Service Company in New York.

65. Footsteps of Blood

On Christmas Eve, 1684, William Blatt's family were at home at Oakwell Hall, Bristall, West Yorkshire, when they saw William walking up the staircase towards the main bedroom. They were somewhat taken aback, for William Blatt was supposed to be in London at the time.

Blatt's wife and children ran up the stairs after him, but, at the top of the staircase, there was no one there. All that could be seen was a single footprint on the floor — it was of fresh blood. William Blatt had, in fact, been cruelly murdered that very evening — in London.

66. The Spectre of Powis Castle

In the 18th century, the ghost of a man in a gold-laced hat often appeared in Powis Castle in Wales. He tried to communicate with the people in the castle but no one took any notice. One day he appeared before a woman while she was spinning, and managed to persuade her to follow him.

He led her to a neighbouring room where he instructed her to lift some floorboards. In a hole under the floorboards she discovered a heavy, locked box. She soon found the key, hidden in a crevice in the wall.

The strange man told the woman that the box and the key must be sent to the Earl of Powis, who was, at the time, in London. The woman did as she was told, and received a handsome reward from the Earl for finding the box. No one saw the strange man in the castle ever again.

67. A Canadian Ghost

Poltergeists themselves are never seen but they make up for that with the amount of mischief they cause. One of the most famous was the spirit that was said to have occupied a two-storey cottage belonging to the Teed family of Amhurst, Nova Scotia, Canada. A ghost calling itself Bob began picking on Olive Teed's 19-year-old sister, Esther Cox, terrorising her in her bed by tearing away her bedclothes, creating the sound of thunder (even though the weather was fair) and causing her body to swell up. Items of furniture would also hover over her as she tried to sleep.

The family called in their local doctor, who immediately found himself a target. On his very first visit, as he bent over to examine Esther, the pillow under her head rose up to wallop him in the face. As he stood in stunned silence, he heard a scratching sound on the wall behind him and turned to see what was causing it. There, in bold letters were the words — 'Esther Cox, you are mine to kill.'

68. A Mysterious Force

When the disturbances first began, in February 1967, Matthew Manning was 11 years old. He and his parents were then living in a house in Cambridge, England. The home was neither strange nor spooky and, being fairly new, had no record of hauntings. But one morning Derek Manning, Matthew's father, noticed something strange: a silver tankard that was always kept on a certain wooden shelf was found lying on the floor. He replaced it, and the next morning it was on the floor again. This strange displacement continued day after day. The children denied having anything to do with the tankard, so one night Mr. Manning carefully dusted the shelf around it with talcum powder, thinking that traces of it would identify the culprit.

The next morning the tankard was again found on the floor, but the powder was undisturbed.

A number of other odd things then began happening, though none of them were spectacular. Objects would be found in places where they should not have been and where they had not been when last seen. At length, Mr. Manning became puzzled and disturbed enough to call the police. They advised him, with constabulary sangfroid, to contact the Cambridge Psychical Research Society. The secretary of the society, Dr. A.R.G. Owen told Mr. Manning that it seemed like the work of a poltergeist and that there was no known cure.

Meanwhile, the disturbances were becoming more severe. Matthew Manning described them several years later in his book, *The Link:*

"Invariably, the objects moved were lightweight ornaments, chairs, cutlery, ashtrays, baskets, plates, a small coffee table and a score of other articles, but none was ever broken or spilled."

As the physical manifestations increased, the house began to produce erratic and unsuspected taps and creaks. The noises would vary from a dull knocking to a sound like a small stone being thrown at the window, and they continued throughout the day and night in all parts of the house.

Dr. Owen came to investigate the phenomena, and he and Mr. Manning posted themselves in the house in the hope of seeing some object being moved by an invisible force. They never did, though things continued to be displaced. Then Dr. Owen told Mr. Manning that there often seemed to be a connection between poltergeist activity and the presence of adolescent children. The three Manning children were sent to stay with relatives, and the mysterious displacements promptly came to an end.

But only for as long as Matthew was away from home. When he returned, the strange phenomena began again, and this time with more vigour. Now furniture and other large objects were moved about and tipped over. Gradually, the mysterious force seemed to weaken. Matthew went away to boarding school, and for a time the poltergeist seemed to have run its course.

The lull was deceptive. At Christmas, 1970, Matthew heard scratching behind the wood panelling in his room and footsteps outside his windows. He went back to school, and there things remained quiet. But when he returned home, the manifestations began again, and this time they acquired a sinister quality:

"I had gone to bed (Matthew wrote)... and I lay there restlessly...I suddenly heard a scraping noise coming from the direction of the cupboard, which continued for almost thirty seconds. Having listened to it for a moment, I switched on my lamp and saw to my horror that the cupboard was inching out from the wall towards me. When it halted it had advanced about eighteen inches. I switched off the light and almost simultaneously my bed started to vibrate violently, back and forth. I was now too timid to move and I lay in anticipation of whatever might happen next. The vibrating ceased, and I felt the bottom end of my bed rising from the floor to what I estimated to be about one foot. The head end of the bed then rose two or three inches, and (at) the same time the bed pitched out towards the centre of the room and finally settled at an angle to the wall."

Thoroughly scared, Matthew went to his parents' room and curled up in a sleeping bag. The rest of the night was peaceful, but when the family got up the next morning, they found the house in a shambles:

"The first room we saw was the dining room. It looked as though a bomb had hit it. Chairs were upturned or simply not in the room, the table was no longer on its feet, and ornaments were strewn around the room and on the floor. The sitting room was in a similar state as was nearly every other ground floor room in the house. Tables and chairs were piled on top of each other, pictures were dismounted, and several objects and pieces of cutlery had vanished."

During the next few days, the pattern was repeated but with new twists: pools of water appeared on the floors throughout the house, and childish scrawls defaced the walls. At the peak of the onslaught the words "Matthew Beware" were discovered; and now, the family saw objects moving without visible assistance, even flying through the air and making 90-degree turns. And if they asked that a specific object be moved to a specific place, the poltergeist would often comply.

This time when Matthew went back to school, the poltergeist accompanied him, first manifesting itself only in his room and then overturning furniture and materialising pools of water throughout the dormitory. Objects would hurtle through the air towards someone, "as if to strike the person, and then either swing away at an angle, just before he was hit, or strike him so lightly that it was hardly felt." The school matron recorded her own experiences of the strange phenomena:

"In my sitting room I might be sitting quietly perhaps sewing, sometimes listening to the wireless, when I am suddenly soaked with coldness, and a shower of pebbles falls from the ceiling. Some nights it may be little chippings of wood which drop into my lap."

At about this time, Matthew discovered what seemed to be a way of re-channelling the poltergeist's energy. He began, first, to undertake experiments in automatic writing and then, in an extension of that activity, to make a series of delicate drawings. He had no idea, he later said, whether these were purely the product of his own mind or whether he might sometimes serve as the medium through which other entities expressed themselves. His guess was that perhaps five percent of his automatic writing might be construed as messages from the dead. Whatever the truth of it was, when Matthew began these activities, the poltergeist phenomena gradually diminished, then finally ceased. Matthew continued his experiments and is said to have developed a number of convincing psychic abilities in the areas of ESP and psychokinesis.

69. The Mummy that Sank the *Titanic*

In 1910, Douglas Murray, an Englishman, bought an ancient Egyptian mummy-case in Cairo. The case had contained the mummified body of a princess who had lived in Thebes in 1600 BC. Just a few hours after he had purchased the case, the American who had sold it to him died mysteriously. Following the American's death, Douglas Murray learnt that the princess had been a member of a powerful religious cult and she had placed a dreadful curse on anyone who dared to disturb her final resting place.

Murray was an experienced Egyptologist and had heard many stories of curses, so he paid very little attention. But then, a few days later, he was on a shooting expedition when his gun went off in his hand. He was so badly injured that his arm had to be amputated from the elbow. Then, on the journey back to England, two of Murray's companions died suddenly. A few months later, two of his Egyptian workers also died in mysterious circumstances.

Murray decided that he must get rid of the accursed mummy-case, and a lady offered to buy it from him. Almost immediately, her mother died, and then her boyfriend left her. When, eventually, she fell desperately ill, her lawyer persuaded her to return the mummy-case to Douglas Murray.

Murray presented the case to the British Museum, where a photographer and an Egyptologist both suddenly died. Finally, a New York museum agreed to take the case and it was shipped to America on a new, 'unsinkable' ship called the *Titanic*. The *Titanic* hit an iceberg and sank, taking with her 1503 people and the dreaded mummy's curse!

70. A Poacher's Hand

Trumpet Major Blandford was a 19th century Dragoon guard who was caught poaching by gamekeepers at Cranborne Chase in Dorset. There was a bloody fight in which one of the gamekeepers was killed. Blandford managed to escape, but his hand was severed in the fight. The hand was buried at Pimperne churchyard in Dorset, where its ghostly form has been seen, searching for the rest of the body.

71. The Haunted Police Station

Police Sergeant Goddard hanged himself in one of the cells of London's Vine Street Police Station early this century. He has haunted the Metropolitan Police ever since. Many policemen have heard him patrolling the corridors at Vine Street Station. He also opens cell doors, and has been known to open desks and examine papers.

72. Phantom Hands

For almost 70 years, a pair of ghostly hands have been scaring people travelling across the Devon moors. In the 1920s, the phantom hands overturned many pony traps.

More recently, people have had the steering wheel of their car plucked from their grasp.

A local resident, Florence Warwick, actually saw the hands clambering across the windscreen of her car. They disappeared when she screamed in terror.

73. A Grandmother's Ghost

Karl Uphoff, one-time rock musician, today believes in life after death. The reason: a phone call from his deceased grandmother, received in 1969.

Karl was eighteen years old when his maternal grandmother died. There had been a special bond between them, and when the old woman grew deaf in her later years, she often wanted Karl's help. Since Karl wasn't always home, she had a habit of calling his friends to find him. And because she couldn't even hear if anyone picked up the receiver, she would simply dial a number, wait a few moments and then say, "Is Karl there? Tell him to come home now." She would repeat the message a few times and then terminate the call, proceeding on to the next number on her list. These calls had ceased, however, two years before her death in 1969, when Karl's sister began taking care of her. Two days after the woman's death, Karl decided to pay an impromptu visit to the home of Mr. and Mrs. Sam D'Alessio in Montclair, New Jersey, whose son, Peter, was a friend of his. Peter and Karl were downstairs in the basement talking when the phone upstairs, rang. The two boys could hear Mrs. D'Alessio talking impatiently with the caller and becoming rather miffed. Karl was stunned when she called down to him.

"There's an old woman on the phone" she yelled. "She says she's your grandmother and she says she needs you. She just keeps saying it over and over."

Karl dashed up the stairs to grab the receiver, but by the time he reached the phone, no one was on the line. But that night, back home, Karl received a series of phone calls. Nobody was ever on the line when he picked up the receiver.

Was the call a hoax of some sort? This possibility seems extremely doubtful. When questioned by an investigator, Karl claimed that none of his current friends knew of the calls his grandmother used to make, and the D'Alessios were recent acquaintances. He also added that he had gone to visit them spontaneously, and that nobody could have known his whereabouts when the call was received.

74. An 18th Century Ghost

Many old theatres are associated with spooky stories. In 1897 the British actor, William Terris, was performing at the Adelphi Theatre in London. One night, as he was leaving, he was attacked and stabbed to death. Since then, his lonely spirit is said to wander through the backstage passages. One actress using Terris' old dressing room even felt a hand squeezing her arm tightly. It left a clearly visible bruise.

The Theatre Royal, Drury Lane in London, is the home of an 18th century ghost in a grey coat and powdered wig. Dozens of cleaners believe they have seen the eerie figure and actors say his appearance is a good luck charm which brings in big audiences.

75. Green Ghost of the Queen Mother's Castle

Searching for a quiet summer retreat, the Queen Mother, Elizabeth of England purchased the remote ruins of Mey Castle on the coast of Mey, Scotland, in 1952. Before the purchase, the Queen's representatives were warned that the ancient structure was haunted by a "screaming girl ghost in green."

"Your panelling and plastics won't stop the haunting!" warned the villagers. Their prophecy was correct. Since restoration, a ghastly green-clad ghost has been sighted on numerous occasions.

The castle was constructed in 1563 by the fourth Earl of Caithness. The nobleman's attractive daughter fell in love with a local farmboy and planned to elope with her lover. The irate father was informed of the lovers' plans and imprisoned his daughter in a room atop the tower of the castle. Heartbroken and grief-stricken, Lady Frances leaped to her death from the tower window. Her crushed body was discovered on the jagged rocks outside the castle.

Reports indicate the suicide is repeated endlessly by the green-gowned ghost. Visitors and caretakers have seen the apparition of Lady Frances gliding ominously up the stone stairway to the tower room. "Tearful moanings and weeping are often heard during the night," said the caretaker.

Nights at the castle have been disturbed by a horrible scream, followed by the cool rush of air, like a body plunging downwards. The phenomena ends with a sickening thud outside the castle. Many people have seen the tower room illuminated at night. "The window was sealed with stone after the suicide," the puzzled caretaker explained. "We can't locate the source of the light."

It is reported that the Queen Mother has not seen the green-gowned ghost. However, royal pets that approach the tower room flee in whimpering terror. The Queen Mother's dogs avoid this section of the castle completely.

Is it possible for an ancient successful suicide to repeat itself endlessly? Many Scotsmen and visitors to Mey Castle swear this frightening manifestation is a reality.

76. The Strange Will

James L. Chaffin was a North Carolina farmer who died in 1921. His family was no doubt surprised and depressed when they learnt the terms of his will. The elderly man left his entire property to his third son Marshall, disinheriting his wife and three other sons completely. The will had been written and properly witnessed in 1905.

Four years later, however, James P. Chaffin Jr. began dreaming that his deceased father wanted to talk to him. He would see the farmer by his bedside, dressed in his old black overcoat; and one day the figure finally said, "You will find my will in my overcoat pocket," and disappeared.

Chaffin was puzzled by the experience, but felt that he should check out the ghost's strange claim. It turned out that the overcoat was in the possession of another brother, so he made the trip to his brother's residence where he found the coat and ripped open its seams. There, hidden in the lining of a pocket was a piece of paper upon which was written, "Read the twenty-seventh chapter of Genesis." Chaffin realised he was onto something, and so he went to his mother's house accompanied by several witnesses, to whom he eagerly told his story. The Bible wasn't easily found but eventually turned up. The book was so dilapidated that it fell to the floor in three pieces when handled.

Thomas Blackwelder was one of the witnesses, and he picked up the portion of the Bible containing the Book of Genesis. He immediately discovered that two pages had been folded together to make a pocket. When he opened it, the surprised witness found a hand-written will dated 1919. It appeared that the deceased farmer had reconsidered, for this new document stated in part, "I want, after giving my body a decent burial, my little property equally divided between my four children, if they are living at my death, and the personal and real estate divided equal and if not living, give share to their children, and if she is living, you must take care of your mammy. Now this is my last will and testament."

By this time, Marshall Chaffin had died and his property was controlled by his widow, so James P. Chaffin took the will to court. Several witnesses testified that the 1919 will was truly in the handwriting of the deceased farmer. Marshall's widow didn't try to fight the case and the small estate was properly redistributed.

77. An Accord

When he was a student in Edinburgh, Scotland, Lord Brougham had a long discussion with a friend about the possibility of life after death. They reached an agreement, that whoever died first would try to contact the other from beyond the grave. When the two men completed their studies, they left Edinburgh and went their separate ways.

Many years later, Brougham was stepping out of his bath when he saw his old friend sitting in a chair. He noted in his diary that the event had occurred on December 19. A few days later, a letter arrived from India, informing him that his friend had died — on December 19!

78. A Famous Ghost

A famous ghost has often been seen walking the ramparts between the Queen's House and the Bloody Tower at the Tower of London.

It is the ghost of Sir Walter Raleigh, the 15th century sailor and explorer, who was imprisoned in the tower for 13 years.

79. The Dreadful Nun

Early one morning, as he was driving from Chippenham to Bath in the west of England, Laurie Newman saw a nun. He slowed down as he passed her, but as he did so, she turned and leapt at his windscreen. Her face was that of a horrible skull!

80. The Ghost of a Balding Man

One of America's most haunted houses is said to be Halcyon House in Georgetown, Washington, DC. It was built in the late 18th century by a naval commander called Benjamin Stoddart, and boasted wonderful views of the Potomac River. Sadly though, Stoddart never found much happiness in his house. His shipping business failed and he was penniless by the time he died in 1813.

From then on, the house has a weird and sinister history. According to legend, slaves died in one of its cellars which was linked by a tunnel to a nearby underground railway. Their moans and cries were heard by house guests, together with the sight of a woman spectre who floated around at night.

The ghost of a plump, balding man has also been seen by several people and seems to match a portrait of Stoddart.

81. Curse on the Kennedy Family

Handsome Thomas Kennedy was a wealthy Scotsman who seldom allowed his extensive land holdings to interfere with his love of fishing. When spring arrived in the Lianachan neighbourhood of Lochaber, Scotland in 1708, he gave instructions to his field foreman each morning and then hurried to his favourite stream to fish.

The tall Scotsman was striding through the tall grass along the amber-tinted river one morning. In the distance, he heard the soft, feminine tones of a song drift through the morning haze. "It was such a beautiful voice that I knew the lass who sung it would be a prize for any man," Kennedy reported.

The Scotsman hurried along the riverbank and discovered a lovely young woman. She sat quietly on a rock that jutted into the river.

The young woman was clothed in a white gown. Her slender hands combed and shaped her long cascades of golden yellow hair. Her feet gently dipped in and out of the cool river water creating small ripples.

"I was very curious as to why such a young girl would be so far into the forest without an escort," Kennedy said. He coughed discreetly, then cheerfully said, "Good morning."

The startled young woman leaped from the rock. She ran desperately into the dense woods. Kennedy was in close pursuit. "Wait! Wait! I mean no harm,' he cautioned. "You're running deeper into the woods and may get lost!"

The blonde girl stopped and turned towards Kennedy. A muddy darkness stirred in the depth of her blue eyes. "I hate all men!" Her shrill scream was an ominous curse. "No good luck will ever come to you, or to any male member of your clan, as long as you live in Scotland. You are cursed!" These ugly words ended in eerie laughter as the girl suddenly vanished from the startled Scotsman's sight.

A troubled Thomas Kennedy forgot his fishing and returned to his home. He knew about the multitude of phantoms and family ghosts in Scotland and Ireland. Although he was not a superstitious man, Kennedy told his family, relatives, and a few friends about the unusual incident.

The phantom lady's curse soon plagued the Kennedy clan. Thomas Kennedy lost a fortune in a fraudulent land deal. One after the other, his handsome sons were stricken with a mysterious malady and died. His daughters married and grieved as they saw the curse pass to their own sons.

Descendants of Thomas Kennedy report that the beautiful phantom appeared just before the death of any clan member. "She clapped her hands and laughed gleefully and predicted a death," they recorded. "When we heard of her visitations, we knew another male Kennedy was doomed!"

Many of the clan left Scotland. Yet the curse seemed to follow them throughout the world. Many people named 'Kennedy' have pondered the ancient curse when bad luck plagues their lives.

82. Phantom Stone-thrower

A nightmare began for Mr. and Mrs. Berkbigler and their five children early in September 1983. They had just moved into their large, but only half-finished desert home when large rocks started smashing into the structure every night. The rocks seemed to come out of nowhere and even the police couldn't find who was responsible. In short, the Berkbiglers were suffering from a rock-throwing poltergeist, a particularly bothersome sort of spook that likes to pelt houses with stones. The family members invariably ran outside to catch the culprit responsible, but there was never anyone in sight. The attacks would usually start between 5.30 and 7.00 p.m. when the family arrived home from their jobs or school. The stones would come in brief flurries and then stop, only to resume. Sometimes the family heard a mysterious knocking on the doors and windows as well.

The Berkbiglers originally felt that a vagrant was responsible for the mischief, but Mrs. Berkbigler was less sure of the cause. "Maybe it's a spirit," she finally told reporters from the *Arizona Daily Star*. "Maybe we've built over some sacred burial grounds or something."

Soon the local press was calling the Berkbigler's problem the "phantom stone-thrower." During the following weeks, the local sheriff's department visited the house and called in helicopter surveillance to solve the mystery. They ended up being struck by the rocks themselves, often in broad daylight, and became reluctant to visit the property.

The most frightening episode of the case occurred on Sunday, December 4. The rocks had been active but sporadic all that day, so two reporters from the *Star* visited the house to interview the family. By 6:10 that evening, rocks were being hurled against the side door of the house with such viciousness that the reporters couldn't leave. The siege lasted for two hours until the family finally called in the police, who escorted the reporters away.

What was so bizarre was that, to hit the side door, the rocks had to travel through the house's open garage. Since a van was parked there that evening, the rocks had to be thrown with uncanny accuracy through a slim, two-foot opening between the garage's ceiling and the roof of the van. Yet the phantom stone-thrower accomplished this superhuman feat without any difficulty!

The case came to its climax on December 6 and 7, when scores of people began showing up at the house to help the family trap the culprit. Despite the constant patrols of the property, the rocks were thrown as usual, picking off people in the pitch black desert with astonishing skill. The self-styled posse succeeded in chasing an intruder from the property, but he turned out to be from the sheriff's office.

But then the rock-throwing simply stopped. The daily sieges ended after the second night of the search, and the case of Tucson's mysterious stone-thrower was left unsolved. It remains so to this day.

83. Phantom Face on the Kitchen Floor

One hot day in August 1971, at Belmez in southern Spain, an old Spanish woman was working in her kitchen when she was startled by a shout from her granddaughter. When the woman turned round to see what the trouble was, she froze in horror. Staring up at her from the pink floor-tiles was a face.

The woman tried rubbing out the face with a rag, but this only resulted in the face opening its eyes wider, as if in great pain and sorrow.

The landlord of the house was called to examine the floor. He ripped up the floor-tiles and put down a new concrete floor. This seemed to solve the problem, but when three weeks later another face appeared on the new floor, the local authorities were alerted and it was decided to dig up the entire kitchen.

Workmen had not been digging for long, when they discovered the source of the phantom face — the kitchen floor had been covering the remains of a medieval monastery.

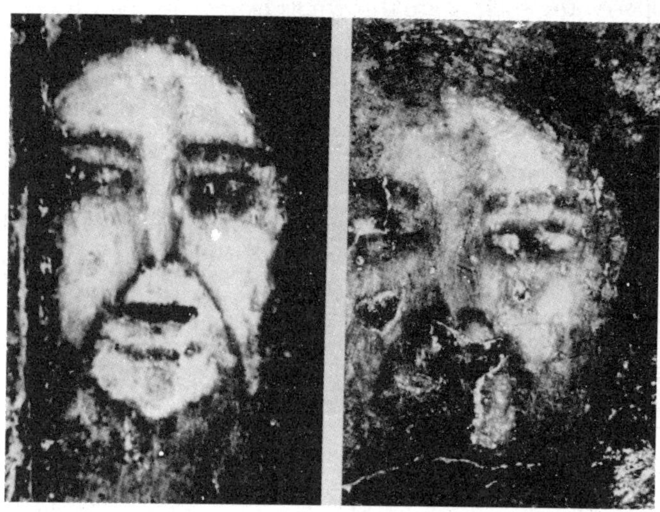

It seems that the discovery of the ancient burial ground only released even more spirits. Ghostly faces began appearing all over the floor, even after more new tiles had been laid, and when the kitchen was eventually locked and sealed up, the faces began appearing in other parts of the house.

A team of ghost-hunters installed sound equipment, which picked up the sounds of unearthly moaning and groaning, but, before a proper investigation could be undertaken, the sounds and the faces stopped, just as suddenly and mysteriously as they had started.

84. A Female Ghost

A female ghost is sometimes seen at the Tower of London. She is pursued by a ghostly executioner who chops off her head. The ghost is said to be that of the Countess of Salisbury, whose execution at the Tower was ordered by King Henry VIII.

85. A Strange Punishment

The ghost of Judge John Glanville haunts Kilworthy House in Tavistock, Devon. Judge Glanville would not let his daughter, Elizabeth, marry the man she loved. Instead, she was forced to marry a goldsmith whom the judge thought more eligible.

With the help of her maid and her lover, Elizabeth murdered the goldsmith. Judge Glanville sentenced his daughter and her accomplices to death. For the past 400 years, Judge Glanville has remained at Kilworthy to haunt the house as punishment for taking his daughter's life.

86. Mysterious Chanting at Beaulieu

When a villager at Beaulieu, Hampshire in southern England, dies, mysterious chanting is heard at Beaulieu Abbey. Several people have heard it, but no one can give a rational explanation for the phenomenon.

87. A Stinking Ghost

Footsteps have been heard frequently in Orcas Manor, near Sherborne, Dorset, in southern England. The ghostly footsteps are often accompanied by a noise which sounds like a body being dragged along the ground. Even after the noise has stopped, there is a lingering, putrid smell that no one can account for.

88. Revenge from an Unquiet Grave

Late one night in 1681, a miller, James Graeme, of County Durham, England, was accosted by the hideous ghost of a young woman. She was drenched with blood and had five open wounds on her head. She told Graeme that her name was Anne Walker and that she had been murdered with a pickaxe, by Mark Sharp acting on instruction from a man named Walker, by whom she was pregnant. She made it clear to Graeme that unless he gave this information to the local magistrate, she would continue to haunt him.

Refusing to believe what he had experienced, Graeme did nothing. But after the apparition appeared, pleaded, and threatened twice more, he went to the authorities with the grisly story. A pit identified by the ghost was searched, and Anne Walker's body was found. Sharp and Walker were arrested, tried, found guilty, and hanged. Anne's spirit, thus avenged, did not appear again.

89. Beloved Wife of King Henry VIII

The ghost of Jane Seymour, the third and beloved wife of King Henry VIII, makes a regular appearance at Hampton Court Palace, the former permanent royal family residence just outside London. She glides through the passageways every October 12, the anniversary of the birth of her son, Edward, in 1537.

90. The Water Diviner

In the late summer of 1929, a new highway was opened to traffic between Bremen and Bemerhaven, Germany. Within a year, more than a hundred automobiles had crashed mysteriously in the highway — all at kilometre stone 239, on a perfectly straight stretch of road. When questioned by the police, survivors described feeling "a tremendous thrill" as their cars reached the marker and said that some great force then seized their vehicles and pulled them off the road. In a single day, September 7, 1930, nine cars were wrecked at the fateful marker.

The police and other investigators were puzzled, but a local dowser, Carl Wehrs, suggested that the mysterious force was a powerful magnetic current generated by an underground stream. To test his theory, he took a steel divining rod in his hand and slowly walked towards marker 239. When he was directly opposite it, and about 12 feet away, the rod suddenly flew out of his hands as if flung by some invisible force to the other side of the road, while Wehrs himself was spun around in his tracks.

Satisfied that his theory was correct, Wehrs applied his own solution to the problem and buried a copper box full of small star-shaped pieces of copper at the base of the stone marker. The box remained buried there for a week, and during that time no accidents occurred. The box was then dug up — and the first three cars that passed the marker were wrecked. The box was quickly reburied, and since then there has been no accident at kilometre marker 239.

Although Carl Wehrs made his living as a water diviner, and presumably knew something about underground streams, local farmers believed that a devil was responsible for the accidents. They said that after it had been exorcised from the road, it entered their radios, which thenceforth produced nothing but static.

91. The Restless Ghost

In the small Illinois town of McLeansboro, a man named Lakey was found dead. His body was discovered by a passerby, his head chopped off, apparently by the axe that was still stuck in the stump next to his body.

No one could understand the crime since Lakey appeared to have no enemies at all.

One day after his funeral, two men were riding horseback near the Lakey cabin site, along what is now known as Lakey's Creek. They had probably gone fishing in the Wabash River and were passing the cabin just as night fell, when they were joined by another, a headless horseman on a large black steed. Unable to speak, the men rode on fearfully, down the bank and into the creek. Suddenly the mysterious rider turned off, moved downstream and seemed to disappear into a pool of water below the crossing.

At first afraid to tell their story, the men soon found that others had seen the same apparition. The ghostly rider's trail was always the same. He joined riders coming from the east, turned near the centre of the creek, and then disappeared.

Today, a concrete bridge carries automobiles over the same spot where riders once forded Lakey's Creek, and motorists have yet to see the restless ghost. The mystery of Lakey's death has never been solved.

92. The Haunted Golf Course

There have been several sightings of ghosts at Howley Hall Golf Club in the West Riding of Yorkshire. Gordon Burney and his wife once saw a strange woman in a long dress appear and then vanish. Another golfer, Tom Gomersall, saw several strange-looking people at the same spot. When his dog ran towards them barking, they too vanished.

One member of the golf club had the strange feeling that he was being watched by a crowd of people on one of the putting greens. He looked around, but there was no one to be seen.

93. Strange Pealing of Bells

At Lime Park in Cheshire, England, the locals often hear a strange pealing of bells. This is usually followed by the grim sight of a ghostly funeral procession. It is said to be that of a young girl who died, heartbroken, when her fiancé died at the Battle of Agincourt, in 1415.

94. Nocturnal Inspection

Captain Bayliss was killed in action in 1915, during the First World War, but for several years after his death, he was regularly sighted by men in his regiment. He was seen astride his beautiful white charger, inspecting the camp at night. One night in 1920, a young soldier, not knowing of the ghost's nocturnal inspections, challenged the captain. When he received no reply, the guard panicked and opened fire — and the ghost of Captain Bayliss was never seen again.

95. Mysterious Manifestations

When a clergyman offered to exorcise the ghost from Mrs. Val Williams's house in St. Asaph, north Wales, she refused, saying, 'You have no right to do that. She was in this house long before we were.'

The ghost was that of a tall, thin woman wearing a white hood. Normally, the apparition, which first appeared in 1970, was seen by Val's twelve-year-old daughter Janthea, but she herself also saw the apparition several times. Strange footsteps have also been heard around the house and objects have moved mysteriously.

Although she was a little scared by these mysterious manifestations, Mrs. Williams always insisted that the ghost should be allowed to stay in the house. But who the strange lady was, or why she haunts the house, Mrs Williams and her daughter never discovered.

96. The Headless Horse

The horrible sight of a headless horse galloping across the moors near Calverley Hall in West Yorkshire has scared quite a number of people. The horse is said to have belonged to Walter Calverley who tried to murder all his family, and who was then executed for his crime.

97. The Phantom Ship

At Forrabury in Cornwall, residents are used to hearing the sound of bells coming from the sea, and seeing the sight of a ghostly phantom ship.

98. Satan's Spirit

"There goes that child again!" snapped Grandma Sybert. "She's jumpin' up and down in her bed again tonight!"

Her son, Frank Sybert, narrowed his eyes and yelled at his nine-year-old daughter, Bertha. "Stop that playin' around and go to sleep."

"It's the spirit, Paw," the child insisted. "He's followed me to bed again tonight!"

A rugged mountain man, Frank Sybert walked into his daughter's bedroom with a determined stride. "I ain't got time for pranks," he said. "I know you miss your mother, child, but..."

The mountaineer's eyes widened as he looked through the gloom of the mountain cabin. The foot of his daughter's bed rose a yard into the air and then crashed to the rough-planked floor.

"I tol' you I wasn't doin' it," sobbed little Bertha.

Frank Sybert cautiously looked under the bed. There was always the possibility that some idle mountain boy had devised a clever prank. There was no one beneath the bed. Incredibly, the bed rose again and levitated higher and higher. The astounded mountaineer flung himself across the bed in an effort to lower it. The extra weight didn't seem to bother the spirit. The bed hung suspended for several minutes while the mountaineer and his family tried desperately to "figger out prank."

For six weeks, Bertha Sybert's animated bed drew curious, mystified mountaineers to the Sybert home on Wallins Creek, near St. Charles, Virginia. Once, several hefty farmers joined Frank Sybert in an attempt to hold the bed to the floor. Bertha's 'Samson's Spirit' lifted them without effort.

After a time, Bertha began to communicate with her Herculean spirit. She would mumble the incantation "sake, sake bib" and the bed would violently bounce around the room.

The unusual phenomena during the winter of 1938 weakened Bertha. Her "spirit" delighted in not allowing the child to sleep. She was covered with bruises — "scores all over my whole body" — when a physician advised the child be taken to a nearby hospital for treatment.

Newspaper reports tagged the tiny mountain girl as "bouncing Bertha."

"I just wish the spirit would leave me alone," the girl sobbed to a reporter from the *United Press.*

Frank Sybert believed it was witchcraft. "If there is such a thing as witchery, I believe my daughter is bewitched," the mountaineer said. "It couldn't be a ghost. It has to be witchcraft because we've investigated every possible source to determine the cause. There just isn't any natural explanation."

After her hospitalisation, Bertha returned home, and the phenomena ceased. Some investigators believe it was the poltergeist phenomena. Many residents of the mountain area believed it was a manifestation of Satan's spirit.

99. The Prime Minister's Ghost

The British Prime Minister, Benjamin Disraeli (1804-81) bought Hughenden Manor, Buckinghamshire, in the summer of 1848. Almost every year from then on, Disraeli and his wife, Mary Anne, retired to the house when Parliament was in recess.

The Disraelis were happy at Hughenden — until Mrs. Disraeli died in 1872. But Disraeli still loved the house and often stayed there in the months leading up to his own death in 1881.

Disraeli's ghost has been seen in Hughenden Manor several times since — usually walking around the upper floors of the house.

100. The Ghost of Queen Elizabeth I

In 1897, the Officer of the Guard at Windsor Castle, Lieutenant Carr Glynn, claimed he saw the ghost of Queen Elizabeth I. She was strolling in the Royal Library. The officer was not the only person to have seen her. Queen Victoria's eldest daughter also saw the ghost of the former queen as have many other people since.

101. The Voices of Long-dead Monks

Mrs. Gertrude Gould was walking past Bramshott Court, a mansion near Liphook, Hampshire, southern England, one evening in 1946, when she heard "a glorious male-voice choir, which came nearer and nearer until it seemed to be over my head." Noticing that the words were sung in Latin, Mrs. Gould assumed that she was hearing a radio playing. But the only radio at Bramshott Court was broken, and the nearest one was in the village, some distance away.

One wing of the old mansion had once been a monastery. Was it the voices of long-dead monks that Mrs. Gould heard that evening?

102. The Dancing Ghost

A most unusual ghost has been reported at Honor Oak Park in Dulwich, south London. Near One-Tree Hill there is a large cemetery, and it is here that the ghost of a young girl appears.

She is said to be in her late teens, and she has long blonde hair. Unlike most ghosts, this young lady appears to be quite content, for she is often seen dancing happily.

103. The Dartmoor Shepherd

David Davies spent 50 years in Dartmoor Prison in Devon. He was given the job of looking after the sheep, and they nicknamed him 'The Dartmoor Shepherd'. Davies died in 1929, but he can still be seen herding his sheep through the Dartmoor mists.

104. A Phantom Coach

According to legend, a girl at Potter Heigham in Norfolk sold her soul to the Devil in the year 1742. She was carried off in a coach by demons, but the coach crashed as it crossed a bridge and all the occupants fell into the river. Each year, on May 31, a phantom coach driven by a skeleton is said to pass over the bridge.

105. A Phantom Bell

Although Rievaulx Abbey, near York, England, was abandoned in 1539 and is now a roofless shell, a heavenly choir has been heard there many times and a bell is sometimes heard ringing. But there has not been a real bell in the abbey for over 400 years!

106. A Mysterious Aeroplane Crash

On March 2, 1948, a DC3 aeroplane crashed on the runway at London's Heathrow airport. Twenty-two passengers, mainly businessmen, were killed. Since that day, a man in a bowler hat has been seen several times standing on the runway.

107. The Headless Coach

At midnight on the anniversary of her execution, May 19, 1536, the ghost of Anne Boleyn travels from the Tower of London to Blickling Hall in Norfolk.

She rides in a phantom coach, driven by headless coachmen and pulled by headless horses. Anne herself sits inside. She, too, is headless.

108. Zack's Curse

The brothers, Zack and Gill Spencer, had been rounding up cattle in Brewster County in Texas, USA. They began to argue over which of them owned one particularly fine looking animal.

Zack allowed himself to get carried away. He shot at his brother and killed him. When he realised what he had done, Zack was grief-stricken.

A cowboy asked how the animal should be branded. "Brand him 'murderer', just like me," said Zack, "and then set him loose, and I hope he haunts the prairies for ever." Zack then buried his brother and shot himself.

From that day in 1890, right through to about 1920, reports of people seeing the bull appeared throughout the land. It was said that everyone who saw it was cursed to become a killer or be killed. It seems that Zack's curse had come true.

109. The Ghost that haunts the Theatre

The ghost of an old lady is often seen in the Royal Box of New Theatre in Cardiff, Wales. She usually appears to be searching for something. Then she walks down the stairs towards the stalls. At a matinee performance long ago, a woman was found dead in the Royal Box — it is believed that it is her ghost that haunts the theatre.

110. A Real Ghost or a Clever Trick?

Many strange things happened in a house at Seaford, Long Island, USA. Bottles of medicine opened on their own, tables fell over and a statuette floated through the air. Investigators were baffled by the case, and to this day it is not known whether the mysterious occurrences were caused by real ghosts or just a clever conjuring trick.

111. The Soldier's Room

During the English Civil War in the 17th century, drunken soldiers murdered a young girl at an inn at Sunbury-on-Thames in Surrey. Visitors to the building, which is now a restaurant, have been terrified by sightings of the young lady. In an attempt to restrain the ghost, 'the soldier's room', where the murder occurred, has now been locked.

112. A Ghost Army

In 1745, a ghostly army was seen walking across Souter Fell in the Lake District in the north of England. This was considered rather unusual, for there had never been a battle in the area, and there was no reason for an army to be marching there. Even stranger was the following report of the sight:

'Carriages were now interspersed with troops; and everybody knew that no carriage had been, or could be, on the summit of Souter Fell. The multitude was beyond imagination for the troops filled a space of half a mile, and marched quickly till night hid them — still marching. There was nothing vaporous or indistinct about the appearance of these spectres.

So real did they seem that some of the people went up the next morning to look for the hoof-marks of the horses; and awful it was to them to find not one footprint on heather or grass.'

113. Thumping Noises

Strange thumping noises are heard in the library at St. John's College, Oxford. They are said to be made by Archbishop Laud, a former Chancellor of the University, who was executed for treason in 1645. The noises are caused by the ghost rolling his severed head along the library floor!

114. Mystery of the Quilt

Mrs. Florence Delfosse was sleeping at her mother's house in Poy Sippi, Wisconsin, USA, when she was awakened by someone tugging at the quilt on her bed. She opened her eyes, but there was no one in the room. Then she heard a voice cry, 'Give me my Christmas quilt!' For three hours she struggled with the unseen person until, eventually, the quilt became still once again and Mrs. Delfosse was able to get back to sleep.

When she told her family of this strange occurrence, her daughter's boyfriend offered to take the quilt to his house to test it. He went home to bed and shortly after midnight, the quilt began to move.

Suddenly, there was a knock at the front door. He went downstairs to answer it. There was a strange man at the door. Although it was pouring with rain, his hat and clothes were dry and he had no face. After a few seconds the man left without saying a word.

The family never solved the mystery of the quilt. It had been found in a box in the house when Mrs. Delfosses' mother had moved there in 1972. Why it moved or who was the mysterious being claiming ownership, they never discovered.

115. Phantom Battle in the Sky

A group of farmhands was walking home from Banbury to Kineton, in Oxfordshire, when they saw an amazing scene at Edge Hill. There, in the sky above, was the Battle of Edge Hill — a battle that had been fought three months previously in October 1642.

The terrified farmhands watched for two hours as soldiers marched across the sky, banners waving, swords glinting. Then suddenly, the scene disappeared.

The men reported what they had seen, and the following day, an investigating party was sent to Edge Hill, only to watch the ghostly battle re-enacted once again.

Later, Charles II sent six of his officers to investigate. They, too, saw the battle, and even recognised some of their comrades who had been killed.

116. The Ghostly Hitchhiker

One evening, Harold Unsworth, a lorry driver, stopped to pick up a hitchhiker who wanted a ride to Old Beam Bridge in Holcombe Rougus, Somerset. As they drove along, the hitchhiker talked, in gory detail, of all the accidents that had happened at the bridge.

A few months later, Unsworth was driving along the same strip of road when he saw the same hitchhiker. Once again, he gave the hitchhiker a ride to Old Beam Bridge, and once again the hitchhiker spoke about the accidents that had happened there.

When they arrived at the bridge, the hitchhiker got out, but asked the lorry driver to wait a few moments while he collected some belongings. The lorry driver waited for 20 minutes, but the hitchhiker did not return, so he decided to drive on without him.

To the lorry driver's amazement, three miles further on, there in the road stood the hitchhiker. Suddenly, he jumped in front of the lorry. Unsworth slammed on the brakes, but although it was far too late to avoid hitting the man, he felt no impact.

Unsworth looked in his rear view mirror, and saw the hitchhiker, seemingly unharmed and waving his fist furiously at the lorry driver. Suddenly, the hitchhiker vanished!

There was only one explanation — the man had to be a ghost. It is thought he was a victim of one of the accidents he had described so vividly.

117. The Phantom Lift

In 1969, the lift in a large hotel in Wales began to move by itself. It would rise from the ground floor and then go up to the second floor. It was first thought to be an electrical fault but when the electricity was turned off, the lift still moved. It even moved when the cables had been cut!

118. The *Flying Dutchman*

The *Flying Dutchman* is the most famous ghost ship in the world. It is usually seen around the Cape of Good Hope, South Africa, and is said to be the ghost of a Dutch ship lost in a storm during the 16th century.

There have been many recorded sightings of the *Dutchman*, but the most impressive one was reported by Prince George (later George V) and his brother, Prince Albert in

July, 1881. The princes described the apparition they had seen as 'a strange red light as of a phantom ship all aglow, in the midst of which light the mast, spars and sails of a brig 200 yards [180 metres] distant stood out in strong relief.'

119. The Vanishing Ship

In November 1941, two seamen were on watch on board the American destroyer, *Kennison*, as she headed towards San Francisco, USA. Suddenly, from out of the fog loomed an ancient two-masted sailing ship. As the vessel passed close to them, the two men could see there was absolutely no one on board. Then the ship vanished as suddenly as it had appeared.

120. A House Flooded by a Poltergeist

In Stuhlingen, West Germany, Elsa Arndt found a small puddle of water on her dining-room floor. She assumed that one of her daughters had spilled it accidentally and mopped it up. But then she found a pool of water on her bed and some more on the bathroom floor.

Elsa believed that her daughters were playing a trick — until water began gushing from the walls! Her husband, Irvin, called in a plumber, but the plumber could find nothing wrong with the plumbing system.

When, one day, blobs of water actually appeared in mid-air, the Arndt family decided to approach Hans Bender, who was well known in Germany for his psychic investigations.

Bender first turned off the water supply to the house at the mains, but still the water came. In one test, Bender had a bedroom completely sealed up, even going to the extent of blocking the keyhole, but when Hans Bender re-opened the room, there was a pool of water on the floor.

After three weeks, with water appearing in the house up to 60 times each day, it suddenly stopped coming. Hans Bender came to the conclusion that the water had been caused by a poltergeist trying to contact twelve-year-old Sabine Arndt, Elsa's daughter.

121. A Great Black Hound

The parson of Blythburgh in Sussex, England, was reading his sermon on August 4, 1557, when he was suddenly interrupted by a crash of thunder. A flaming arrow pierced the church wall and the church bell crashed to the ground, followed by tumbling masonry. The congregation was terrified, but there was more horror to come — a great black hound of massive proportions came rushing through the church, attacking people as it went.

The hound vanished and was never seen again, but its burnt and blackened paw marks can still be seen on the old church door.

122. 23 Years Ago

As he walked towards the Fox and Hounds Inn near Northampton, one winter's day in 1940, George Dobbs saw a car coming along the snow-bound road. Approaching the car from the opposite direction was a man on a bicycle. The man appeared to have no head.

The car driver did not seem to see the cyclist, but continued to head straight towards him. Within seconds the car had passed. George was convinced that the cyclist must have been hit, and he ran over to help. But the cyclist was nowhere to be seen!

When he arrived at the inn, Dobbs told his friends about his strange experience. Then one of his friends, the local gravedigger, said, 'There was an accident at that spot 23 years ago. A cyclist was knocked off his bike in deep snow — the accident severed his head.'

123. The Ghost of Lady Ann Streatfield

The ghost-woman on horseback, who frequents the village of Chiddingstone in Kent, is quite unusual. This is because she is normally seen in daylight, riding through the village. She is said to be the ghost of Lady Ann Streatfield, who lived in the local manor house in the 18th century.

124. The Last Will

Nine days after his father's death in May 1948, Leslie Freedman had a strange dream. In the dream he saw his father, Leonard, sitting at his office desk. His father turned towards him and said, 'I want you to call all the family together at 7 o'clock on Saturday.'

Leslie Freedman was not sure what to do about his dream, but he called the family together as requested — although he dared not tell anyone the reason for the gathering.

By 6.50 p.m. everyone had arrived at the house and they sat in the dining-room next to the library, and waited for Leslie Freedman to explain why he had called the meeting.

Suddenly, the whole family found themselves looking through the open door into the library. There, looking at some books, was the ghost of Leonard Freedman. The spectre pointed to one of the books and then vanished.

It was Leslie's brother, Arthur, who moved first. He went into the library and took out the book that the phantom had pointed to. It was *A History of Lighthouses on the Irish Coast.*

Arthur flicked through the pages in curious amazement. Inside the front cover was Leonard Freedman's last will and testament — a document that the family had been searching for, ever since his death.

125. The Haunted Jacket

For the play *The Queen Came By* at the Duke of York Theatre in London, actress Thora Hird had to wear a long dress topped with an embroidered velvet bolero jacket. Whenever she wore it she experienced a choking sensation. Her understudy experienced the same sensation when she wore it, as did the stage manager and the director's wife.

The jacket proved to be quite a problem. Three mediums were called in, but to no avail. Three members of the cast were asked to try the jacket and two of them felt as if they were being choked by it.

After some research into the history of the jacket, a Victorian original, it was discovered that the owner had been throttled to death by her lover while she was wearing it. She had haunted the garment ever since.

126. The Valet's Ghost

On the night of May 31, 1810, the Duke of Cumberland had returned to St. James' Palace, London, after a visit to the opera, when his valet, Sellis, tried to kill him. The attempt was unsuccessful. And, later that night, Sellis committed suicide.

That, at least, was the duke's version of events on that fateful night. However, it was not long before rumours began to circulate that Sellis had, in fact, been blackmailing the Duke of Cumberland, and that the duke had actually murdered him.

It seems that this rumour may well have been the truth, and the Duke of Cumberland's version of events a lie. For, since that night, the valet's ghost has been seen several times — sitting up in his bed with his throat cut!

127. The Most Haunted Village

Pluckley in Kent, in the south of England, is said to be Britain's most haunted village. It is believed to have no fewer than 12 ghosts. These include the Red Lady, searching for her lost baby, the White Lady who glides through the library of Surrenden Dering manor house, and a horse-drawn coach that careers down the village street. There is also the ghost of an old pipe-smoking gypsy woman, a phantom schoolmaster who hanged himself, and the black shape of a miller. It is also said that the ghost of a colonel who hanged himself walks through the woods, and terrible screams are heard near the railway station where a man was smothered to death. A phantom monk has been sighted at a house called Greystones, a ghostly lady haunts Rose Court, and a mysterious modern ghost inhabits the church of St. Nicholas. At the appropriately named Fright Corner, the gory death of a highwayman who was killed by a sword and speared to a tree is said to be re-enacted every night.

128. Untimely Death

The Fleur de Lys Inn at Norton St. Philip, Somerset in the west of England, has been haunted for the past 300 years, ever since an innocent passer-by was tragically killed there. The man arrived at the inn to find that an execution of rebels, who had supported the Duke of Monmouth's uprising in 1685, was about to take place behind the premises. As he opened the gate to let the men through to the execution site, he was pushed into their midst by a guard. He was hanged by mistake, and his ghost is a constant reminder of his untimely and unfortunate death.

129. An Unusual Gift

Whilst he was visiting Luxor, Egypt in 1890, Count Luis Hamon was called upon to attend a prominent Arab sheik. Hamon was well known as a psychic healer and he had been asked to cure the sheik of malaria. This he did, and the grateful sheik gave him an unusual gift in return. It was the mummified hand of an ancient Egyptian princess.

The princess's hand had been cut off by her father, King Akhnaton, in an argument. Hamon offered the hand to various museums, but no one was willing to accept it, so it was eventually locked away in the safe in Hamon's London home. It remained there for over 30 years, until, one day in 1922, Count Hamon's wife opened the safe to find that the hand was no longer shrivelled. Its appearance had changed to a healthy-looking living hand.

The Countess insisted that the hand should be disposed of immediately, and her husband readily agreed. It was decided that the hand should be given a proper funeral, out of respect for the dead princess. This was arranged for the night of October 31. During the funeral service, Count Hamon laid the hand in the fireplace and then read a passage from the *Egyptian Book of the Dead.* Suddenly, there was a clap of thunder and a blast of wind blew open the door to the sitting-room.

In the doorway was the figure of a woman dressed in the traditional clothes of an Egyptian princess. Her right arm had been severed. The figure approached the fireplace, bent over towards the hand, and then vanished!

When the Count and Countess recovered sufficiently from their fright, they searched the fireplace. The hand had vanished, and it was never seen again.

130. The Helpful Ghost

The ghost of Nance is often seen by lorry drivers travelling to York in northern England. She runs alongside the moving lorries, and if there is any danger ahead, she slows them down to warn them.

Nance was an 18th century farmer's daughter who left her fiancé to marry a highwayman. But the highwayman was already married. He left Nance pregnant and penniless. Nance's ex-fiancé, a coach driver, found her several months later, standing on the York road nursing her baby. He took her home to care for her, but both she and the baby died. Because of the coach driver's kindness, Nance's ghost has been helping drivers ever since.

131. The Ghost Castle

Built in 1905, by the Roland B. Lane family, the house on Franklin Avenue became the Mecca for the ghosts. An old family friend called Irma, returned from the grave and took up residence on the second floor of the house, where she now plays for visitors. Her repertoire can be surprisingly contemporary at times — even Britney Spears' songs have been heard on occasion!

There is also another ghost in the house. Apparently one of the magicians once died on stage and is still seen in the theatre where he last performed.

132. The Electric Girl

On January 15, 1846, Angelique Cottin, a girl from La Perrier, France, developed a strange problem which bothered her for 10 weeks and earned her the nickname "electric girl", and then just as promptly, left her. It so used to happen that when she went near objects, they whizzed away; chairs refused to be sat on, her bed rocked when she lay in it and the table recoiled from her touch.

References

1. Petes Eldin, *Amazing Ghosts and Ghouls.* 1987
2. Warren Smith, *Strange Women of the Occult.* 1968
3. Charles Berlitz, *World of Strange Phenomena.* Vol. I & II. 1989
4. Peter Haining, *Ghosts, Illustrated History.* 1974
5. The *Reader's Digest, Mysteries of the Unknown.* 1985
6. Peter Underwood, *Haunted London.*
7. *Fortean Times,* No. 34, Winter 1981, p-16.
8. *The Unexplained, Mysteries of Mind, Space and Time,* Vol. 3, Issue 32.
9. D. Scott Rogo, *The Poltergeist Experience,* pp. 261-268.
10. F.S. Edsall, *The World of Psychic Phenomena,* pp. 12-13.
11. Frank Smyth, *Ghosts and Poltergeists,* p.60.
12. William G. Roll, *The Poltergeist,* p.38.
13. Charles Fort, *The Complete Books of Charles Fort,* pp. 577-81.

14. Andrew Mackenzie, *A Gallery of Ghosts,* pp. 139-41.
15. Charles G. Harper, *Haunted Houses,* pp. 116-20.
16. Robert Dale Owen, *Footfalls on the Boundary of Another World,* pp. 333-40.
17. Raymond Lamont Brown, *Phantom Soldiers,* pp. 80-81.
18. The *Reader's Digest,* Eds., *Folklore, Myths, and Legends of Britain,* pp. 106-107.
19. Mary Bolte, *Haunted New England: A Devilish View of the Yankee Past,* pp. 43-46.
20. Edmund Gurney et al, *Phantasms of the Living,* pp. 493-94.
21. Philip Van Doren Stern, *The Breathless Moments.*
22. Matthew Manning, *Poltergeist.*
23. Several Issues of *Fortean Times.*
24. Gyles Brandreth, *1000 Horrors, The Most Horrific Book Ever Known.* 1983
25. Jenny Randles, *Paranormal Source Book.* 1999
26. Mike Dash, *Borderlands.* 1997
27. Ian Wilson, *Life After Death.* 1997
28. Hilary Evans, *Visions, Apparitions, Alien Entities.* 1984
29. Loren Coleman, *Curious Encounters.* 1986
30. Celia Green and Charles Mc Crecry, *Apparitions.* 1975
31. Richard Davis, *The Encyclopaedia of Horrors.* 1987

32. Karen Farrington, *3-D Masks, Monster.*
33. Nigel Blundell, *Facts or Fiction, The Supernatural.* 1996
34. John Guy, *Ghosts, Haunted Houses and Spooky Stories.* 1999
35. T.C. Lethbridge, et al, *Ghosts and Ghouls.* 1961
36. J.A.Brooks, *Ghosts and Legends of the Lake District.* 1988
37. John Spencer and Tony Wells, *Ghost Watching.* 1994
38. Colin Wilson, *Poltergeist.* 1993
39. Thomas Allen, *Possessed.* 1993
40. Thurston Hopkins, *Adventures with Phantoms.* 1958
41. Elliot O' Donnell, *Twenty Years Experiences as Ghost Hunter.* 1996
42. Daniel Cohen, *The Phantom Hitchhiker.* 1995
43. Colin Wilson, *Afterlife.* 1987
44. John and Anne Spencer, *Encyclopaedia of Ghosts and Spirits.* 1992
45. Christina Hole, *Haunted England.* 1990
46. Paul Hamlyn, *Larousse Encyclopaedia of Mythology.* 1959
47. *Time Life, Phantom Encounters.* 1987
48. John G. Fuller, *The Ghost of Flight 401.* 1978
49. The *Readers Digest's Book of Strange Stories, Amazing Facts.* 1975
50. Guy Lyon Playfair, *This House is Haunted.* 1980

True Stories of World Famous Series

More Books on World Famous Series

More Books on World Famous Series